UNCOLOURED

BY CHARLES AZULAY

One Printers Way
Altona, MB R0G 0B0
Canada

www.friesenpress.com

Copyright © 2024 by Charles Azulay
First Edition — 2024

Editor — Richard Dionne

ISBN
978-1-03-916098-9 (Hardcover)
978-1-03-916097-2 (Paperback)
978-1-03-916099-6 (eBook)

1. BIOGRAPHY & AUTOBIOGRAPHY, PERSONAL MEMOIRS

Distributed to the trade by The Ingram Book Company

For my beautiful daughters Jessica and Cameron, who are an inspiration, and whose unconditional love is my continued source of strength. It's a privilege to be your dad.

For my little sister Gina, my partner in crime who's been looking out for her big brother since the day she was born.

For my husband Rodel, who encouraged me to tell my story.

And for my parents Jack and Jan, whose courage, persistence and love pushed me to keep singing and dancing through life.

TABLE OF CONTENTS

1

HOME 7

2

THIS IS ALL VERY NEW TO ME 25

3

PITY THE CHILD 43

4

I GUESS THIS IS GOODBYE 57

5

THE MUSIC AND THE MIRROR 65

6

I HOPE I GET IT 83

7

RAINBOW HIGH 93

8

ON THE RIGHT TRACK 111

9

CLIMBING UPHILL 129

10

WHAT I DID FOR LOVE 139

11

SOMETHING WAS MISSING 151

12

WE DO NOT BELONG TOGETHER 163

13

KNOWING WHEN TO LEAVE 171

14

LOOKIN' GOOD, BUT FEELIN' BAD 183

15

I AM WHAT I AM 193

16

UNEXPECTED SONG 205

1

HOME

Of course I would trip up the steps to the front porch of the house. Christ, I thought. Are these things ever going to get fixed? It had been seven years since my mother first noticed the cracks in the concrete, but my father always had a reason why he'd get to it tomorrow.

I brushed the gravel from around the freshly made hole in the knee of my jeans, and noticing the front door was open, I went inside and announced my arrival.

Almost nothing in the house had changed since I'd been there last. Everything seemed meticulously in its place. The curtains of the bay window in the living room were open just enough to let in an almost perfect amount of early afternoon sunlight.

After removing my shoes at the front door, I made my way into the living room, past the grandfather clock which stood imposingly next to the staircase. Its constant ticking and quarterly chimes were something I'd grown to ignore when I lived here, but now, its heavy tone seemed soothing, as if it were an old friend sensing the apprehension in my movements as I made my way into the house.

Rounding the corner, I found the kitchen empty, so I made my way back to the stairs to announce my arrival once again.

The familiar baritone of my father's voice finally shouted down from his office; he'd be down momentarily. I knew unequivocally that this meant he was going to be a while, so I went into the living room to wait patiently.

The large bay window overlooked a rose garden, and as I stood looking out, I had a clear sightline to the multitude of cars that drove past the house daily. A lot could be seen from that window, including a large part of my childhood. The garden led to a long front yard, and at the end of that, near the sidewalk, stood the tallest tree on the block. Garth Street at Mohawk Road was a busy intersection on the West Mountain of Hamilton, so kids in the area had to be very careful when going out to play.

My parents bought this house new when the neighbourhood was built in the late 1960s. This particular model, a brick two-story with a built-in garage and four bedrooms, was impressive to me as a child, but as I grew older, it became a very common middle-class suburban home.

Much like the cracks in the front steps, my dad took his time fixing and updating the inside of the house as well. Sure, the last forty years had seen the old green shag carpet that ran throughout the house pulled up, and the avocado-coloured appliances swapped out for beige ones in the '80s. But otherwise, most of the house remained as I'd always remembered it.

Although quite faded and peeling at the corners, the beige flowered wallpaper that I helped my dad put up in 1980 still hung in the hallways between each room. And the bathroom, which featured the same pattern only in white-and-pink flowers, still sported its original pink toilet, sink, and tub from the year the house was built. "Why replace something that's in perfectly good working order?" my dad would say. And who could argue with that?

The house felt quiet and calm as I sat down on the sofa and continued looking out at the garden. I began thinking about the things I'd wanted to say to my dad, but laughed at the idea of him sitting down to have a heart to heart.

"What are you worried about?" I could hear a gentle voice say, and I turned to see my mum standing by the living room entrance. She seemed shorter since I saw her last, but then again, I thought the same thing every time I'd visit. Her hazel eyes sparkled in the sunlight, and at almost eighty years old, she still radiated a youthful glow. I would often tease her that I'd never seen a little old white lady look so good. In fact, the only thing that gave away her age was her bright silver head of hair, which had grown a little long now, forcing her to move it repeatedly from in front of her glasses.

"Everything's fine," she said.

"I wasn't overly concerned," I replied, but of course I was. I was rarely summoned to the house, and when I was, it was never for anything good.

My mother took a seat across from me in her favourite wingback chair, and took a sip from a glass containing a very generous pour of what I could only assume was the finest cabernet to be boxed locally.

"You know your dad and his obsession with organization. He found some things that he felt you might need, or that you might want to hold onto."

I was pretty sure we could have done that over the phone, but since I was there, I was more than happy to take a look at what there was.

"So, how are you doing?" she asked.

I wanted to tell her that everything was good, which it was for the most part, but I would have been lying if I said I wasn't still struggling.

"Not bad, actually. The clinic is running well, so that keeps me pretty busy."

It wasn't exactly a lie, but I definitely didn't want her to know that I was still having a little difficulty. Although work in my massage therapy practice had been pretty steady, I also had massive debt from my student loan which, if I'm honest, had been giving me more than a few sleepless nights.

"Are the girls managing alright?" she asked.

"Yeah, they're pretty resilient. They miss you," I said, wishing I would have brought them around to see her more often, but I'd been so busy with work that I barely had time with them myself.

My mum flashed me one of her big supportive smiles before taking another sip from her glass.

"I know," she said. "I miss them too."

My parents never complained about not seeing their granddaughters that often, they were just happy to see them when they could.

I really thought that leaving my acting career would allow me more time for visits with them, but I'd been overextended at a job with a lengthy commute, not to mention that I lived more than an hour away from their house.

Casually, I headed into the kitchen. "Is there any ginger ale?" I asked.

My mum raised her voice slightly in an effort to make sure I could hear her. "I think so. It'll be on the bottom shelf of the fridge if there is, but there's beer in there if you want."

She was blissfully unaware of my recent five years of sobriety, so in order to avoid that conversation entirely, I simply told her that it was a bit too early in the day for me.

As I sat back down on the sofa, I noticed next to me what I assumed was the reason I'd been summoned.

"Is that it?" I asked.

"Oh yes, it is," she replied, acknowledging the old box which sat at my feet. "There's been so many trips up and down the stairs, I'd forgotten it was already down here."

It was a very old bankers' box; the kind with the lid that simply lifted off the top. And though it brandished a printed label with my name, I'd never seen it before. These same type of boxes could be found all over the house, and they were filled with anything and everything you could imagine. Both my parents were hoarders in some way, but with his OCD tendencies, my dad made sure that everything that my mum held onto was boxed up neatly and clearly labelled.

I was a little afraid of what I might find inside, but decided to ask her anyway.

"Should I just go through it?"

"I don't see why not."

The box looked almost new and showed no signs of dust; a clear indication that it had been recently removed from the bottom of a much larger pile. After removing the lid, I was taken aback to discover what appeared to be a carefully archived personal history. It was complete with important documents that were sealed in clearly marked envelopes, and although most items were fairly recent, others dated back to my childhood.

Unlike my dad, who saved things that he thought might come in handy later, my mum had a history of saving anything she felt had the slightest bit of sentimental value. So, I found myself facing into a life's worth of souvenirs that had been kept in pristine condition.

There were pictures, playbills, and newspaper articles, many of which were duplicates since my mum would often ask for the programs or ticket stubs from any of her friends that had seen me in a show. Although it felt like a lifetime ago, these items of memorabilia were reminders of a very unique moment in time when pushing boundaries helped create some of the most groundbreaking musicals in the 1980s through the 2000s.

Having been in shows like *Les Misérables, Miss Saigon, and Cats,* as well as plays at the Stratford Festival of Canada, it was difficult to overlook the fact that I had been a part of many of the productions that helped shape a generation of musical theatre into a much more interestingly diverse landscape.

As I sifted through the box, I became more and more ambivalent, intrigued, but somewhat hesitant. I wasn't sure if I should look much further in case I discovered something that would result in an emotional response I wasn't prepared to have.

Yet my curiosity got the better of me, and as I slowly removed the envelope marked "ADOPTION," I began to wonder what I'd find. Inside were a few documents with my personal information that had been given to my parents by the Children's Aid Society. The familiar light-blue folder was something I'd seen many times before, and I was happy to find that still taped to the inside cover was the only newborn picture of me in existence.

It's funny how I hadn't really changed that much. My almond-shaped eyes, brown skin and the dimples on both cheeks, all were the same. Of course, my little tuft of curly dark-brown hair had filled in nicely since, and I was lucky not to have lost very much of it even into my 40s.

Immediately overcome with emotion at the image of myself at my purest moment, I felt a sense of peace. However, as I continued to read through the folder, I became aware that it was a feeling that wouldn't last.

These documents from the CAS were more or less an assessment of my pre-adoption experiences. I had undergone some medical as well as psychological testing to determine my overall health, and even though I seemed mostly unaffected by the circumstances that led to my stay in foster care, I struggled with my emotions and had difficulty trusting adults. Physically I appeared fine, with the exception of the injuries to my genitals which, although described in the report, were not explained in any great detail. This was all information that would be important for any prospective parents to see prior to adoption. As I continued to scan through some of the documents, I could see by the expression on my mum's face that she was genuinely concerned.

"Are you okay?" she asked.

"Of course," I said. "I'm fine."

I wasn't. I'd been caught a little off guard, and hoped she hadn't noticed the crack in my voice as I tried to appear unaffected.

Among some photos tucked in the back of the folder, I came across a black-and-white snapshot of my little sister and me that was taken at the last of the foster homes we'd lived in. With only a year between us, it was easy to see how people thought we were twins as we got older. We had the same dark complexion, and similar smiles, but as a little girl in the 1970s, her dark curly hair was being grown out long.

I loved that photo because it was the perfect representation of our relationship dynamic. We were sat next to each other on the chesterfield, and although I was trying to smile, I was making an awkward face because my sister's fist was making contact with my right eye.

Laughing a little, I placed the photo to one side. There were several that were taken that same day, and each made me feel a connection to a youthful, albeit short-lived sense of innocence. Chasing my sister around the coffee table. The two of us finding eggs in a barn near one of the foster homes. The irony of being sick with chicken pox, and then being forced to eat chicken soup. So many memories and emotions came flooding back, it was hard not to feel overwhelmed.

It was a difficult position I had put myself in. Sorting through these memories would no doubt stir up old feelings, as well as spark some conversations that I was certain my mother was not ready to have.

As a child, and through my teens, I'd lived through some unpleasant experiences that eroded almost all my self-esteem, and even though I survived abandonment, and sexual abuse, the trauma left me shattered, and lacking a sense of self-worth. Everyone experiences trying times during their childhood, and I was no different. But I think that being raised by a family with such significant cultural differences caused many of the emotional problems I had throughout my life.

Growing up, I'd always been told how lucky I was to have been chosen by my parents, and that I should be grateful that they adopted me and gave me such an amazing life. Truth was, at the time, I didn't feel lucky. And I definitely didn't feel grateful. I was conflicted as I struggled with my sense of identity, and no matter how much my parents tried, I rejected them and refused to conform to what I thought they wanted me to be.

A non-practicing Jewish father and a Protestant Scottish immigrant mother living in a working-class steel town and raising two mixed black children, seemed like a sitcom in the making, but looks can be deceiving. I was being raised by quite possibly the whitest people in Canada, and for me, therein lay the problem. Our differing opinions on how important race would be throughout my life became the catalyst for a multitude of issues I had with my parents that went far beyond just teen angst and rebellion against them. It led to a full-on attempted coup d'état, leading to my eventual exile.

"Some things I remember about these photos, and some I don't," I said, the tremble in my voice almost certainly betraying my efforts to look calm and composed.

There were definitely situations I would have been too young to recall, and the social workers written account of what led to my abandonment didn't spark anything in the way of a concrete memory. For the early things, the images were hazy, but I could still sense the emotions I felt then, some of which were so intense and overwhelmingly vivid that my eyes began to swell with tears.

My mum continued to sip from her glass, seemingly unphased by my unintended emotional release.

"You were a cute kid," she said, breaking up some of the tension.

"Yeah, I was," I asserted, and we both kind of chuckled.

The kid in those photos *was* cute and appeared to be a normal, happy, healthy little boy. Though in reality, he was confused, mistrusting, and desperate to be loved.

As the grandfather clock struck one in the afternoon, and started its pronouncement in chime, it's melody combined with the appearance of this unchanged room made me feel as though time had stood still.

Being raised in a white family impacted my life in ways I never could have predicted. So did the pain of abandonment as well as what I'd been exposed to in the foster system. My mother had some idea of what my sister and I had been through before her and my dad came into the picture, but the broader parts of the story were muddied over time. Whatever the facts, there was one thing for certain; the cards were stacked against us from the beginning.

We were born in St. Louis, Missouri, in the early 1970s to a French-Canadian mother and an African-American father. This in itself already presented a number of challenges. Cities around the United States had been experiencing a change, and St. Louis was no exception. It was the height of the Civil Rights Movement, and white and black youth everywhere were still pushing for equality and an end to racial discrimination.

It had been only a few years since schools were officially desegregated, and even though discrimination based on race in public facilities had only just been deemed unlawful, my parents' interracial relationship was not looked on too favourably.

In order to escape the volatility of their relationship, my birth mother left my birth father, and took my sister and me to Canada where, after a few short months, she realized she lacked the capacity to look after us on her own. In what I can only imagine was an act of sheer desperation, she left us with a babysitter one afternoon and never returned.

Tragic circumstances aside, I had always been somewhat sympathetic towards the poor babysitter who was left in that situation. Not only did she have to figure what to do with the two children that had been left in her care, but she was more than likely left unpaid, and without so much as a reference.

I spent a great deal of time in the foster system, and the experience was, to put it politely, disturbingly unpleasant. My sister and I were moved at least once because of neglect, from a home where we were often locked in a closet to keep us quiet and out of the way.

It's something I could barely remember, having only been around two years old, but it was known to our social worker, who obviously documented it in an attempt to have us relocated. Although I couldn't remember how it felt to me as a small child, thinking about it later in life filled me with an immeasurable sadness and an anger that was difficult to let go of.

Our last foster family was a much better fit for my sister and me, and although I have no real recollection of what they looked like, I could sense the emotions I'd felt around them. Our foster mother gave me a sense of comfort which led me to believe that she was kind. But when it came to our foster father, I felt a strong sense of fear. He may have been very strict with me, or perhaps just not overly patient, but the feeling is associated with one of the only distinct memories that I'd had about my time there.

It was more of an image really, but it was one that stood out because of that intense feeling of fear I'd experienced. I'd hidden from our foster father under a chair in the kitchen of their home, and though most memories of the past were a little cloudy, the image of that Sears dinette set from the 1960s with the flower-patterned high-backed chairs was crystal clear.

"Look at these photos!" I said to my mum. "You'd never know how close we were."

I displayed a constant need to be with my little sister, and I'd become extremely upset when they tried to separate us for any length of time.

"If I noticed that she wasn't around, I would throw a huge temper tantrum."

"I can just imagine," my mum said quite confidently, as she'd seen my temper firsthand.

My sister and I *were* however separated at bath time, which created an entirely new level of discomfort for me. It was painfully upsetting to have one of the older foster children constantly touching what I'd always been taught was my "private area." At such a young age, I never thought of it as being sexual, but because I knew that letting someone touch me in that way was wrong, I was terrified I'd get in trouble if our foster parents were to find out. The thought of it made me angry and upset, and the more I stared into the bankers' box and at its contents, the more upset I became.

"You know, if anything like what happened to me, I mean being touched in that way, had happened to her, I'd never be able to forgive myself."

My mum and I had never really spoken about it before, but I chose to be blunt in order to get a clear and honest reaction from her.

"We never really knew what happened to you," my mum said, quite visibly upset at my candid revelation.

"That's because we never talked about it. All the evidence was there in the report from the Children's Aid."

I fully expected that my mum would feign ignorance about what had happened to me. After all, "If we don't talk about it, it never happened," could have been the slogan on our family crest. At first, I thought perhaps this stroll down memory lane wasn't such a good idea, but in the moment, it felt so good to say some things out loud. This was a conversation I didn't expect to have with my mum, but there we were. There were things she may not have known about the traumatic events which caused me to act out in such anger as a child, but I wish she had wanted to learn about them as a way of helping me work things out.

In foster homes around the country, a blind eye had been turned to what some children were being subjected to. There was definitely plenty of blame to go around, and though some would argue that the foster system was broken, sadly, it was working exactly as it was designed. The screening process for foster families had improved over time, but I suspected that in regards to dealing with Indigenous children, or children of colour, there was still a significant amount of bias and discrimination.

"Do you remember when you decided to adopt?" I asked, as though I didn't already know the answer.

"Of course I do," she replied. "Why?"

"No reason," I said.

I thought back to the story that my mum had told me years earlier when I'd asked her the same question. I wasn't surprised when she explained to me then that since her and my father already had a girl, they wanted to adopt a boy. What was interesting was finding out that their initial plan was to adopt a child left behind from the Vietnam War.

Years later, I would encounter a very famous photo of a Vietnamese woman handing off her young daughter to American soldiers at Vietnam's Tan Son Nhut airbase. It was during the fall of Saigon in 1975, around the same time my sister and I were adopted. The photo appeared on the inside cover of the book of musical selections from *Miss Saigon*. It served as Claude-Michel Schönberg's and Alain Boublil's inspiration for writing the Broadway show, in which I went on to play a lead role for over 1,800 performances. The image was powerful, and looking at it in relationship to my own story, I imagined myself being passed on to another family, in hopes of a better life.

When inquiring about overseas adoption, my parents were persuaded to focus on children living in Canada as there were so many in need of good homes. My sister and I had been declared wards of the Crown in the middle of the "60s Scoop" era when many Indigenous children were forced into foster care to be adopted out to white families. This was a time when there was a concerted effort to assimilate those children through rampant transracial adoption around Canada.

Because we weren't a part of that specific demographic we had a slightly easier time. It was quite normal for the CAS to place children like myself and my sister with what they considered a "stable and loving family," which was just social services' speak for "white." This practice had the potential to yield some socioeconomic benefits, but not without significant cost. It was clear in most cases that the connection to the child's culture would inevitably be severed.

In our case, the CAS, in what was a fairly progressive stance for the time, suggested that the family we were placed with should have ties to the black community. My adopted father's older daughter with his first wife was also half black, and more than likely the reason the CAS greenlit our adoption.

What my parents did in adopting my sister and me was commendable, especially since at that time, most people were looking to adopt newborns, or small babies. We were three and four years old respectively, and it was very difficult to find a home for an older child, let alone siblings who were children of colour.

It was just the way things were, and unfortunately, when it came to adopting children outside of their race, a family's good intentions could easily become the stones with which an unimagined road to hell is paved.

Now that there were some subjects out in the open, I felt things were about to get a bit deep and perhaps a little emotional. With my father still working away upstairs, I decided to divert the conversation slightly in order to lighten the mood.

"It must have been our award-winning performance on television that made you choose us," I announced, to which I anticipated a laugh from my mum. She didn't disappoint.

My very first television appearance was with my sister on a program designed to draw attention to children in need of homes, and in particular, Indigenous and children of colour. It didn't get me my SAG card, but it was cool to be on TV regardless. The show was called *Family Finder* and featured the Beatles song "All You Need Is Love" as its theme.

Its format was similar to that of an animal shelter ad, but what it lacked in the way of celebrity activist hosts and dispiriting soundtrack, it more than made up for with the visuals of dejected looking children joylessly paraded in front of a camera. It had all the benefits of a humane society infomercial, without the looming threat of being put down (I think).

The show targeted a very specific demographic, similar to the World Vision segments on Sunday morning television. Designed to stir up feelings of white guilt in middle-aged couples with decent financial resources, producers hoped that a few of them would take a kid or two off their hands.

"It was Big John who brought us on the show that day. Do you remember him?" I asked.

"Of course I do," my mum remarked.

There was no forgetting the man we jokingly referred to as "Big John." He was the social worker assigned to our case. I remember him as an older gentleman, but in hindsight, he was probably fairly young. There was a kind-hearted quality to the man. He had a big smile, and I was forced to lean my head way back to see it because of his extraordinary height. Even through the frames of his glasses, I could see that his eyes, a shade of brown that matched his hair and beard, were sympathetic and caring.

He would often drive us around in his green Volvo station wagon to the many appointments we had, including the first meeting with my parents.

"He brought us to meet you at the mall that time when you brought us those gifts," I reminded her.

I could almost see my mother's memory of that moment as I watched her try to conjure up an image of that day. We met my parents and their older daughter at a local shopping mall where we congregated around a bench seat in front of one of the stores. Our then-prospective parents gave me a little toy racing car, and my sister a little bean-stuffed doll that she'd lovingly, and somewhat unimaginatively, referred to as "Beanie." I remembered how special and important it made me feel being allowed to keep that toy car for myself. Anything we'd had at the foster homes were communal, and so my sister and I had no toys of our own. Not having to share with anyone else made me feel empowered, and so that little car became something I held onto into adulthood.

My parents' older daughter seemed nice, and at the age of fifteen she had over ten years on me. While she too was biracial, and the link to the black community on which our adoption approval was based, the fact that she rejected any hint of her blackness made that link all but inconsequential. She had a pale complexion, and light-coloured eyes. In fact, apart from her dark curly hair, nothing about her features suggested anything other than Caucasian. For reasons unknown, she preferred to "pass" rather than embrace her true ethnicity. I can only assume this decision was due to low self-esteem, and a strained relationship with her birth mother. I'm sure these same feelings also contributed to her choice of partner, who was the very definition of toxic masculinity.

Like a lot of young girls in the 1970s, she married right out of high school to her long-time boyfriend. He was the type of guy whose failed aspirations of playing professional hockey left him desperately clinging to the remains of his teenage athleticism, and a once-loyal hairline. Marrying so young meant that we would only live together in this house for a few years, so to say we grew up together would be a bit of a stretch.

In my adult life, I'd always tried to figure out my older sister's indifference to her ethnicity, and the great lengths to which she'd gone to hide that part of who she was. I was never sure if it was something that happened over time, or if she'd always been that way. Whatever the reason, her behaviour always felt to me like a bit of a slap in the face, and something I would never really understand.

"No way!" I shouted, nearly causing my mum to jump out of her seat. "I thought this had broken years ago."

I could hardly contain myself as I unwrapped the tissue paper from around a little ceramic Christmas ornament that my mum had made. It was a beautifully painted little boy in ice skates, holding a wrapped present behind his back. At the bottom was written "Christmas 1975."

"This was from our first Christmas with you."

My mum seemed surprised at how happy I was to see this little keepsake. I'd never been one to hang onto too many knick-knacks or collectables, but this was very special. Not only did it symbolize our first Christmas as a family, but it happened to coincide with the finalization of our adoption as well.

When all the paperwork had been signed that year, my sister and I travelled to our new home – this home in Hamilton where I was now sitting a lifetime later. It was already mid-January of 1976 when my parents drove us from Ottawa in their AMC Hornet station wagon with the faux wood panelling because of course, it was the 1970s. On the roof they'd tied their most recent gift to us: the extremely popular and equally nauseating Sit & Spin, a toy that enticed kids to sit on it and spin around until they became too dizzy to stand, vomited, or both.

At one point during the drive, I'd awoken from a nap in time to look out the car window just as we were driving up a hill. At the top, I looked out at the lights of the city below, and immediately for me, this became the image of our new home.

I don't think I'd ever seen anything like it in real life. It was like an artist's rendering of a big-city skyline used as the background for a movie. I must have fallen back asleep, because when we arrived, my dad had to carry my sister and me into the house one at a time, to put us to bed.

Originally, we were supposed to arrive before Christmas, but due to some legal paperwork issues, that time frame was pushed to the new year. Because of that delay, my parents decided to keep up their Christmas decorations in anticipation of our arrival. They prepared food, put gifts under the tree, and joined by all their friends, they held a second holiday celebration in order to give us something we'd never experienced before.

The excitement of all the gifts and attention was overwhelming, but it lasted only for a brief moment. Once things died down, and we tried to settle in is when I started to become very anxious.

Change is never easy, and as could be expected, the transition to our new home and family wasn't a smooth one, at least not for me. It was difficult to navigate where and how I would fit in, and like with the cracked concrete of the front-porch, I was going to have to tread lightly at first, until I figured out my safest path.

2

THIS IS ALL VERY NEW TO ME

I'd moved the box to the dining room table, and almost instinctively sat in the place where I ate as a child. I continued digging around inside and pulled out a few more ceramic pieces, each one putting a smile on my face. They made me recall how my mum used to go to her ceramics class every Thursday night and how my dad would complain that he'd be stuck with what he called "babysitting duty." Since we were his kids, I can only assume he was talking about what we now refer to as "parenting."

"Are you sure these are for me?" I asked. "I'd really like to be able to touch them without fear of retribution."

I looked over at my mum completely deadpan, and watched her burst into laughter. She knew exactly what I meant.

Not long after our arrival in Hamilton, I was scolded by my mum for having broken a ceramic figurine she'd made. She tried to be gentle. In fact, I'm almost certain she didn't even raise her voice. She had a way of maintaining her composure, often using catchphrases or speaking in riddles that seemed more like advice than reprimand.

As we stood in the finished basement of our new home, she'd suggested that I think carefully before I touched anything. "Is it yours? Is it a toy?" she advised me to ask myself, and if the answer was no to either of those questions, then I was to keep my hands off.

There seemed to be an awful lot of rules for a five-year-old kid, which gave me reason to dislike my new situation even more. I didn't want that place to be my home, and so I tried to convince myself that it was just another temporary spot where we'd been forced to live. Without hesitation, I snapped back at my mother, who at this point was really more like a stranger to me. I told her that I hated her, and couldn't wait to move away.

There was no reason to think that I actually hated her. I was just a scared kid who was upset at pretty much everything. Upset at the instability, and from being removed from the foster home and the family that we'd become used to. I was vulnerable, yet cautious, and felt the need to test her limits to see how long this new arrangement was going last.

After that awkward exchange, I knew that these new adults were going to be of the "no nonsense" kind. In fact, my mum would continue to prove this time and time again.

Garth Street was extremely busy, and we were given a warning the first time that my mum let us outside to play. She told us, "If you put one toe on that street, you're in for it." Of course, I took that as a challenge, and decided to put her to the test. As we were playing outside, I decided to look around to see if anyone was watching. Once I thought the coast was clear, I went down to the street and literally put one toe on it. My mother, who had been covertly watching from the living room window, immediately came storming out of the house, grabbed me by the ear, and dragged me back inside. I never saw it coming, but I knew then that I needed to rethink my strategy if I was going to get away with anything living in this new house.

Unsurprisingly, I didn't get a spanking, since the pleasure of doling out the punishment was reserved for my dad. That's probably one of the reasons I'd always been a little more cautious around him.

Nevertheless, I continued to test the waters with my parents to see what it would take for me to be shipped off to another home. It was clear, however, that I wasn't going to get the reaction I'd anticipated, and so finally one day, when I'd had enough, I went to the basement where my sister was playing and told her we were leaving. I intended for us to run away, and without hesitation, she came with me.

It was a cold and windy spring day, so we bundled up and set off down the street, mindful of course not to step onto it for fear of another motherly reckoning. Having nowhere to go on our side of the street, and because we couldn't cross to the other side, we ended up walking back and forth in front of the house, where I knew my mum could see us. Of course, I would glance back at the window from time to time hoping to catch a glimpse of her looking as sorry as I told her she'd be.

My mum continued to watch us from that tell-tale living room window, and figured we'd get tired after a while. And when we finally did, and subsequently went back inside, she said nothing, and just made us a hot lunch.

I felt a little better in that moment as I alternated between mouthfuls of Campbell's tomato soup and a grilled cheese sandwich that had not only been made with love, but with real cheese, as my mother deemed anything processed to be a crime against nutrition.

Knowing that I was angry and frustrated, she understood that I'd been testing her. So in an effort to earn my trust, she never spoke a word about running away. She simply warmed us up, and fed us, as if nothing had happened. This didn't mean that the testing was over. There would be much more of that to be sure, but after being shown such kindness and understanding, I settled into the idea that my new mum and dad might actually be okay.

Once I started school, things became a little easier. I began to socialize with other kids my age, and I eventually got used to the idea that like it or not, I was with this family for the long haul.

Some of the kids at my school I knew from the neighbourhood, and it didn't take long for me to make a friend. A.J. was my age, and lived across the street from us, and like me, he liked sci-fi and fantasy movies, as well as comic books that featured heroes with superpowers. He was also the only other black kid in the neighbourhood, and I naturally gravitated towards him.

Hamilton was not very visibly diverse then. The steel industry drew a lot of workers from Western Europe, and the city became a haven for many new Canadians, but there were almost no Asian or black families in our area. I rarely saw anyone who looked like me, and if I did, they at least had parents that seemed to match.

A.J. and I hung out as often as we could, playing at each other's houses, although I always felt more comfortable when we'd hang out at his. The smells of Jamaican cooking coming from his mother's kitchen were heavenly, and I often wanted to stay over there and eat with his family.

It's not to say that my mum's cooking was terrible. She was an incredible baker, and the cakes and cookies she made, especially around the holidays, were the stuff of legend. However, her British post-war cooking style left her meals somewhat tasteless and bland. The roast we would consume as a family on Sunday evenings was always well done, and my mum would boil the living shit out of any and every vegetable she served. This removed any shred of evidence they'd contained any nutrients let alone flavour. It was for this reason that when playing over at my house, I was always too embarrassed to ask A.J. if he wanted to stay for dinner.

Because we shared a love of superhero comic books, he and I traded them back and forth all the time. The thing was, that until I'd met him, I'd never seen a single comic that featured characters of colour. He was the one who introduced me to Marvel's *Luke*

Cage and *Black Panther,* and I was captivated by each and every issue. These were heroes I could look up to, and aspire to be like one day. Heroes that looked like me.

We had such an affinity for our comics and we would read them repeatedly from cover to cover. The only thing we may have loved even more was *Star Wars,* which, thanks to my mother, we were able to see. She actually stood in line with us for almost an hour waiting to get into the Tivoli Theatre, the only movie house in Hamilton where it was showing.

Our obsession with anything *Star Wars* related ran so deep that the only real fight A.J. and I ever had was when we forgot to consult one another, and ended up at school on Halloween both dressed as Lando Calrissian. Unfortunately with so few black role models, Lando was the most popular character at the time.

When my older sister moved out of the house and I was taking over her room, my parents completely redecorated it in a *Star Wars* motif. At the time, my younger sister and I were spending a week with my grandparents at their cottage in Sauble Beach. When we returned, my new room had been transformed into every eight-year-old boy's dream. From the wallpaper to the bedding, it was the perfect backdrop for some classic battles against the evil Galactic Empire.

Leafing through a few more photos, I came across one of our family on vacation in Barbados. I immediately showed it to my mum, who almost lost a mouthful of wine, something I couldn't imagine she'd be able to forgive herself for.

"What in the world?" I asked.

When she took a much closer look, she didn't seem as bothered.

"Actually, I'm not half bad," she said, now seeming almost proud of how she looked.

"But what about Dad?"

"Hey," she said. "It was the '70s."

It was 1978, to be precise, and we looked like the most bizarre group of misfits ever to be assembled under one roof. My sister and I were extremely dark, because we'd been in the Caribbean for over a week, and unlike the white folks around us, we didn't need sunblock. My parents seemed to be giving off a *Three's Company* vibe by serving up some Stanley and Helen Roper "realness." And although I didn't remember that exact shade of my mother's hair dye, I was all too familiar with my father's perm and the deep V-neck shirt he wore to expose his majestically groomed porn star chest hair.

What was interesting about the photo was how out of place my parents looked. They were two white people in a sea of black and brown faces, and I couldn't help but wonder if in that moment, they might have experienced how it felt to be different.

Placing the photos aside, I started to question how so much stuff could have been packed into one box. I wasn't just pulling out photos and papers, but ribbons and trophies too. That said, I'm not ashamed to say that the ribbons I received from playing on some team sports were mostly for participation.

Growing up in Hamilton, athletics were encouraged, and there was no shortage of recreational sports outside of school. My parents signed me up for the usual things for kids my age. I played T-ball for a while, then moved up to playing on a little league softball team. I was actually a pretty good player, and even though it was a lot of fun, it was only during the summer months and thus a limited activity.

Still, I preferred activities that weren't as athletic. This might have been one reason I was a bit of a chubby kid, something that my older sister's husband seemed to delight in teasing me about at all those flavourless Sunday dinners. In fact, my brother-in-law never let up with his constant commentary on my weight, and as hard as I tried to slim down, I was constantly forced to endure his snide little comments which I'm sure he thought were very clever at the time. His go-to was forcibly grabbing my chest, and declaring that my boobs were getting bigger than my little sister's, a comparison which begged the question – what was he doing looking at my little sister's chest?

What infuriated me was that my older sister never did anything about the things he said or did to me. Then again, why would she? She never said a word about how he treated my little sister, which although arguably was far worse than how he'd treated me, it was never my story to tell.

My weight had become a real issue, even though I was young and hadn't really had a growth spurt yet. At least most people who were tactless enough to comment simply chalked it up to baby fat. As I held the photo of my softball team "The Hamilton Firefighters," I was reminded how difficult it was being an overweight kid, and just how much of my childhood was spent focused on it.

I'd always suffered from a very low sense of self-esteem, but the 1980s really seemed to kick things up a notch.

"I don't look as fat as I thought I was," I indicated, as I showed my mum the team photo.

"You were stocky," she said. "But you eventually grew out of it."

"Not in time to get the cool clothes like most of the other kids," I replied, still bitter that I never got to sport some of the more fashionable trends of the time.

Once softball season had ended, and the summer would start to wind down, I was inevitably forced into an activity that ate away at my very soul; the indisputable humiliation of back-to-school shopping. My mum would take me straight to the boys' department at the back of Sears, and there, tucked away in the corner like a dirty little secret, was a section where people like me could find a pair of pants.

Spoiler alert! Companies back then weren't overly sensitive when it came to marketing. Labels were fairly blunt, and did their best to tell you exactly what you were buying without any polite descriptions.

"God, those stupid jeans you made me wear," I said with the feeling of shame as fresh as if it were 1982. "The brand patch on the back said 'Husky' right on them. You might as well have pinned a 'Kick Me Hard' sign right to my back before sending me off to school."

"I remember having to take you there, practically kicking and screaming," my mum recounted as she tried to hide her laughter. She knew it was horrible, but let out a few giggles as she continued to recall. "I couldn't even get you to come out of the changing room."

"I was mortified. The kids at school were so mean."

All I wanted was a pair of designer jeans like *Sergio Valente* or *Jordache,* that were all the rage at the time. Instead I was forced to wear what looked like the remnants of a denim circus tent, simply because I had bigger thighs and a bigger ass than other kids my age.

To make matters worse, I had been forced to attend a youth diet centre. It was basically an after-school fat camp for kids that my parents insensitively referred to as "The Chub Club." It was a humiliating experience having to weigh-in before getting into a pool to do aquafit with the seniors from the local Jewish community centre.

All of the dieting became so stressful that eventually I started to break out in a rash all over my body, so the doctor recommended that my mum stop being so overly concerned about my weight. It was important to encourage me to be active, but obsessing over it was proving to be counterproductive.

Not having to count calories every minute of every day was a relief, but at the time, I hadn't realized the damage that had already been done. I'd developed a terrible relationship with food that was extremely difficult to break away from.

Being chubby, but also wearing glasses made me a target for bullies at school. As a result, I tended to act out in class. Students were often left to handle any playground discourse on our own, and my lack of critical thinking skills at that age made it difficult to stand up for myself. Of course in a school setting, children were discouraged from resorting to violence regardless of the situation, but that didn't stop a lot of them.

I was pushed around, and called every name in the book just for being different. Fatty. Nigger. Nerd. All my personal favourites were hurled at me by boys and girls alike, and having little to no self-esteem already, it didn't take much to push me over the edge. Sure, I was overweight and near-sighted with glasses, and didn't fit in with the other kids at school, but to top it off, I felt like an outsider in my own home. A black kid whose real parents didn't love him enough to keep him, who had to be taken in by strangers who didn't even look like him. And even though I was a child, and not yet at the point where I was questioning my sexuality, I was a boy who wasn't very interested in sports, which gave way to speculations that the other kids ran with and thus, "faggot" was added to their repertoire of insults. It's no surprise I chose to be angry at the world, and to be defiant towards some of my teachers. Like other adults in my past, I felt that they too had abandoned me when I needed them the most.

Some teachers could see the pain through my mask of anger, while others were complicit in painting me with the brush of "troubled kid," making it easier for them to justify their unwillingness to deal with me.

With this newly designated identity, I found myself in the cigarette smoke filled principal's office more times than I cared to remember. Sometimes for a strict talking to, but several times for the strap, which was doled out pretty casually by our principal. Again, the 80s.

Between the trouble at school, and my waning athletic enthusiasm, I felt the need to find activities to enjoy on my own. Like most kids my age, I loved television, and I was drawn to shows that were musical. I'd been a fan of the Saturday morning variety shows, and reruns of *The Hudson Brothers Razzle Dazzle Show* were by far my favourite.

Standing on our toybox playing air guitar, I was captivated by the music. I would become the frontman, looking cool, and showing off my mean guitar skills as the studio audience went crazy. It made me feel special and important, and I knew then and there that I wanted the experience of garnering that kind of respect and attention. I was obsessed. And because I was so enthusiastic about learning to play, or more likely because I wouldn't shut up about it, my parents decided to get me a guitar. They also set up some lessons with a local gentleman who taught out of his house.

I was excited to play, but at that age, I was only interested in one thing. Learning the intro to *Stairway to Heaven*. Unfortunately, my teacher was more into technique and theory than teaching classic rock guitar riffs. I continued with the lessons for a while and seemed to have a natural talent for it, but after a while, I became impatient. If I wasn't going to be a rock star in ten easy lessons, then I figured it was a waste of my time.

Although I'd quit my formal lessons, it didn't deter me from learning Zeppelin's gorgeous rock intro, and eventually the whole song. That sense of achievement led me to spend hours listening to numerous artists and teaching myself to play by ear. Over a fairly short period, I learned how to use chording, and even accompany myself while I sang. When I heard a song that I wanted to learn, I would practice tirelessly until I got it. My mum and dad were quite surprised and impressed that I was able to continue learning on my own and they were more than happy to have me continue with something that I showed so much interest in.

Fortunately, I also had a grade school music teacher who played a vital role in helping me explore my musical talents. She was an amazing teacher, and a skilled pianist who was more progressive than most teachers at that time. In her class, she always had us singing some of the most popular songs of the time. It was only years later that I'd come to realize just how amazing she really was.

She rocked out on that school piano to Three Dog Night, Cat Stevens, and even Jim Croce. At one point she taught us music from the 1974 television film, *Free To Be...You and Me.* It was based on an album by Marlo Thomas and Friends, and to me, it was life altering. It tackled social issues like racism, as well as issues within the feminist movement. The message was one of love and acceptance, and I couldn't get enough of it.

The music was inspiring for sure, but the message was so important to me. My emotions ran high when listening to those songs, and learning about the inequities that existed in our society. Because of *Free To Be...You and Me,* the seeds of moral and social obligation had been planted, and would grow into my empathetic desire to help others.

I'd taught myself a few of the songs from the movie while honing my guitar skills, and for a while became hyper-fixated on putting together a decent repertoire. Although I'd never really thought of myself as much of a singer, it didn't stop my mum from forcing me to entertain her friends at parties. I would regale the guests with the songs of Gordon Lightfoot and John Denver, with my sister singing harmonies to duets that required them. We had a few songs from *Free To Be...You and Me* that were standards for us, but somewhat ironically, The Paul McCartney/Stevie Wonder song *Ebony and Ivory* was our most requested. We did try to take our little act on the road, but only ever made it as far as the recreation room at my grandmother's seniors building, where we had a standing gig on weekends.

Many people thought I had a natural ability to sing, and so I would perform whenever I got the chance. The attention I drew was good for my self-esteem, but I also started to associate my talents with my value as a person. I was treated differently when I performed. Even my own parents seemed more interested in me, or at least interested in showing me off in a way that made them proud. This made me feel like I'd found the key to being accepted and even admired, and a way to ensure that I would always be seen.

In third grade, my school had introduced a music program for strings, which allowed students to learn violin or viola for three years, after which time, they could keep the instrument. It was something I really wanted to do, so my mum went ahead and signed me up.

My sister started her violin lessons the following year when she was old enough, but I'm not sure how much she enjoyed it. She was the one who was more into sports, and kept herself busy with ringette in the winter, and baseball in the summer. Even though she definitely had musical talent, I wasn't entirely sure that it was her thing.

For some reason, the violin came naturally to me, and my teacher quickly pushed me into playing at levels much higher than beginner. Every year, I'd compete in a local music festival, where I'd won several gold medals that my mum proudly had framed. Eventually, I played both violin and viola for The Hamilton Youth Philharmonic Orchestra, which I loved, even though it took up a lot of time.

My Saturday morning orchestra rehearsals were some of my fondest memories. I was actually with a fairly diverse group of kids, and I had friends who were white, black, and Asian. We all loved music, and we enjoyed diving into some Mozart and Beethoven, as well as the odd Beatles tune. Our conductor was pretty cool, and we were often heard rocking out to his orchestral arrangements of music by more contemporary artists.

I was well liked by our conductor, so rehearsal was one place where I didn't act up too much, although as a kid, I sometimes couldn't help myself.

One day while I was subbing in for a viola player, my friend and I were goofing off while the conductor was working with the second violins. We were playing some pop song while holding our violas like guitars, when out of nowhere, the conductor's baton suddenly came flying straight at my head. I guess I'd been pushing my luck, so I quickly learned to save the fooling around for after rehearsals.

I loved being in a group of kids who all shared a love of music, and even more, I loved the attention I was getting at home. I was being noticed, mostly by my mum, and whenever there were awards or concerts that won me praise, she felt on top of the world.

Unlike the majority of parents who had difficulty getting their children to practice an instrument, mine had a hard time getting me to stop. I would spend hours in my room with my violin, feeling a sense of freedom as I became swept up in the excruciatingly passionate tones pouring from my instrument. My proficiency with the violin made me aspire to play for the Hamilton Philharmonic Orchestra. In fact, it was my dream for quite a few years, and as I became more disciplined in my studies, it became a very tangible goal.

As young as I was, I still understood that it was a career that wouldn't lead to fame and fortune, but I was thrilled at the idea of working at something I loved to do.

"Do you remember the phone company scam Dad had going?"

"What do you mean?" my mum replied.

"You know, when I needed to tell him to pick me up from orchestra rehearsal. He'd get me to call collect, and…"

"He wouldn't accept the charges," she finished. "He'd hang up and come get you."

What a cheapskate, I thought to myself, although truthfully, on a musician's salary, I would more than likely need some of those penny-pinching strategies that were classic Dad.

Music had become such a huge part of my life, but my growing obsession with classical music left little room to explore other genres of artistic expression. That was until my mum saw an audition notice in the local paper looking for kids my age.

At ten years old, I auditioned for the musical, *The King and I.* The show required children with singing ability, that could play the royal princes and princesses of Siam. Since my sister and I had spent a lot of time singing and performing, musical theatre seemed like a natural progression.

There were tons of children and parents there, and even though it was something I had become quite used to doing, singing in front of a large group of strangers was quite different from doing it in front of a small group of family and friends. I managed to keep my focus, as I patiently sat and waited my turn to sing *Happy Birthday,* as all the kids were asked to do that day. The creative team was seated at the table, but the director got up and moved in closer so she could hear the children better. Having her stand so close seemed to put the kids more at ease while we sang in front of everyone. When it was my turn, I managed to control my nerves as I sang out as strong and clear as I could.

My sister and I were both chosen to be in the show, and as a celebration, my parents took us out to The Ponderosa Steak House, one of a few places we went to celebrate special occasions. Dining out was a fairly common occurrence for my family, especially on a Friday night, but our choices were limited as my parents were both pretty frugal. My mum loved the all-you-can-eat salad bar, and more importantly, my dad loved anywhere kids ate for free. It also didn't hurt that he could light up a cigarette right there at the table as soon as he'd finished his meal, something my sister and I hated. My father had been a smoker for years, but gave it up in the early 1980s, although not without a fight. Even after quitting, he continued to consider himself a smoker. Much like an alcoholic not drinking, he was a smoker who was choosing not to smoke.

That production of *The King and I* was an eye-opening experience, in more ways than one. The show had a primarily white cast, with my sister and I being the only people of colour. During the performances, the white actors would cover themselves in dark makeup, and use eyeliner to achieve a more "Oriental" look. At the time, I thought nothing of it because the people around me, more specifically my white parents, didn't see it as a problem at all.

From the stereotypes to the racist makeup, none of what I experienced in that show was acceptable. And although it did give me a chance to discover theatre, it foreshadowed some of the ways in which I would be limited simply because of the colour of my skin.

When I was just starting out as an actor in 1990, most roles for people of colour were limited to racially stereotyped characters created by white writers in a white context. As a result, I became frustrated at constantly being called in to audition for "Gang Member #1" or "Thug #2."

It was never lost on me that I'd experienced a certain amount of white privilege because of who my parents were, but without them to fight for me in the adult world, I learned fairly quickly that I had certain disadvantages that I was not at all prepared for. I would have to learn to navigate the world I was living in through my brown eyes, but not without significant difficulty and sometimes great disappointment.

Expressing myself through theatre provided me somewhat of an escape, because at least onstage I was able to be just about anything. More importantly, I didn't have to be me, which I appreciated because considering how I was already viewed by those around me, I'd begun to resent who I was.

After the closing of *The King and I*, I enrolled in a summer program run by Theatre Aquarius, a small professional theatre company operating out of Hamilton Place, the large theatre complex in the heart of the city. At age eleven, and not really into sports anymore, this program provided me an opportunity to do something I really enjoyed for a large part of the summer. The school was created by the artistic director of Theatre Aquarius, and its principal was a well-known local dancer and choreographer.

Theatre Aquarius is where I got the chance to test the limits of my artistic abilities among a group of other kids with similar interests. It was there that I discovered dance, and I became fascinated with everything to do with it. It was like attending a summer school version of the television series *Fame,* and I was doing my best to nurture my inner Leroy Johnson.

At the end of the summer, I decided to study dance with the principal of the school at his studio in the east end of the city. It helped me become more comfortable with my body and gave me the confidence to tackle some of my insecurities at a time just before starting at a new school.

In my move to junior high, my biggest decision was what instrument to play in music class. All the options were wind instruments, and since I had no experience with any of them, I decided almost at random. I knew that whatever I chose I would have to carry home, and when I realized all the flutes had been assigned, I opted for the clarinet, since it was the next size up.

My music teacher who was someone I admired immensely, convinced me to join the after-school band, and because of his patience and support, I was able to realize some of my untapped musical potential.

A fresh start at a new school was exactly what I needed to show people that I wasn't the problem child that I'd been in elementary school. I was liked by the teachers as well as the other kids, and was able to become an A+ student, thanks in part to the confidence I'd gained from music and dance. I became known for my musical talents in band, and even ended up conducting a Christmas concert in eighth grade. Our music teacher had been off sick, but instead of cancelling the performance, and letting all our hard work go to waste, the band members asked if I would lead them.

It was wonderful to feel successful at school, but at the same time, any anxiety or pain that I was suppressing started to manifest itself at home. My life in public seemed normal, but at home, the cracks were slowly beginning to show. I began to feel that no matter how hard I tried, I couldn't control my anger which was now being misdirected toward my parents, and causing some serious conflict.

I often thought that my sister was the favourite and could do no wrong. That's not to say it was true, it was simply my perception at the time. After all, I was the one who constantly challenged authority and was always in trouble. My parents became extremely frustrated with my constant need for attention, and though I was certainly a needy kid, it was probably because I struggled with such insecurities.

In elementary school, I chose negative ways to attract attention, but in junior high, instead of acting up at school, I took my anger and frustration out on my parents.

I'm not really sure when I began to show signs that I was losing control, but arguments with my parents came often, and were the primary source of my stress and anxiety. They often stirred up feelings of my past in foster care and my anger would build to such grand proportions that it was difficult to manage. My behaviour left my parents concerned and uncertain how to handle me.

It wasn't just the past, (which was difficult enough to deal with), but there were things that I started to notice about my parents that caused me a great deal of frustration as well. As I grew older and developed friendships with kids of all different backgrounds, I started to feel less and less like I belonged with my family. Everyone

I met seemed to have a real connection to their roots with stories and traditions passed from generation to generation. I yearned for more understanding about who I was and where I came from. Unfortunately, my parents' inability to help me in that capacity gave way to my feelings of invisibility. These new feelings were very difficult to process and although I felt resentment towards them, I struggled to understand why. Eventually I came to understand that race had played a much larger part in the fracturing of our relationship than I had expected.

White people tend to feel uncomfortable when it comes to discussing race. I'm not sure why, because there needs to be conversation for one to gain understanding of a perspective different from their own. With my parents, those conversations were only ever superficial, which was unfortunate because there were definitely things I wish I'd been able to say. As a teenager, I never really knew how to articulate my feelings productively, but I never shied away from speaking my mind while trying.

I had serious trust issues with white people, and given my past, it was easy to understand why. From the beginning, when it came to anything important in my life, they were the ones making all the decisions. No matter the situation, they were injected into the equation and as a result, it was at their hands that I had suffered the most.

Maybe it's because I'd grown older and become more aware of my surroundings, but I definitely noticed some of the subtle, and not so subtle displays of prejudice held by each of my parents. In hindsight, it was those attitudes and behaviours, the stereotypes and constant microaggressions, that would shape much of our future family dynamic.

3

PITY THE CHILD

"What's Dad doing upstairs?" I asked, walking back from the kitchen having grabbed another ginger ale.

"Oh, you know him, he's going through a bunch of receipts because of the change in how he has to file his income tax now."

"Maybe he should be here while I go through this stuff, he might want to reminisce."

I was being facetious of course. I couldn't fathom my father being sentimental in any way. He just wasn't that guy. He wasn't known to open up and talk about his or anyone else's feelings, period. Even growing up, I never really saw him express much emotion. Honestly, I don't think I saw him enough to have gotten a real sense of who he truly was. When I was a kid, a man could live at home and still be a kind of absentee father. This is how I'd always viewed my dad. He'd come home from work, and one of us kids would get him a beer so that he could relax in his chair while he waited for dinner to be ready. As we sat at the table to eat, children were seen and not heard, and no one was talking about their "feelings."

My mum, on the other hand, loved to look back on the past. I knew that it had been her who held onto the bulk of the nostalgia found in this box, most likely in the hope that I would want to revisit the old days. It was her way of holding onto some of the good memories when times weren't so easy. Like my mum, I could be sentimental, but I did my best to use my memories of the past as a way to learn from my mistakes and move forward. I wish that Mum could have done the same, because although well intentioned, some of her attitudes made things extremely difficult for me growing up.

"What the hell was that thing you told me when I was little? You know that thing about why people were different colours."

"What are you talking about?" My mum was clearly confused by what I was asking her.

"The thing about God, and the oven," I said.

"I don't know what the hell you're talking about, but whatever it is, I'm sure it isn't true."

My mum had this idea that if you forgot something you were going to say, that it must have been a lie. I never knew where she got that from, but I assumed it was one of her superstitions from the old country, like the ones about putting shoes on the table, or leaving a hat on the bed.

"Oh, now I remember," I said, suddenly realizing how ridiculous the whole thing really was. Not long after my sister and I were adopted, my mum once tried to explain to me why we were different. I'm not exactly sure why, because at five years old I was quite self-aware.

My mum was a regular church goer, so anecdotes of a more religious or at the very least, spiritual nature, were not uncommon. She started to explain that, "When God was baking people..." What the hell? Okay, I had no idea where she was going with this, but I knew it most definitely couldn't be anywhere good. "When God was baking people, some were burnt, some were underdone, and some came out just right." I assumed the burnt folks were black, and since she pointed at herself when she said it, I deduced that white people were underdone. That left the "just right" people, who were supposed to be my sister and me because of our golden-brown complexions.

Now, in her own sweet way, and on the surface, it was a nice attempt to help me understand why we all weren't the same, and to let me know that there was nothing wrong with being what I was. It was, however, a troublesome way of dealing with something as important as my identity.

I'm not sure if my mum was under the impression that I didn't really understand race, but I had lived through so much in my short life that I was acutely aware of who I was, and how I came to exist.

She wanted me to be comfortable in my own skin, but unfortunately, wasn't addressing the actual issue, which was the fact that I would be treated differently than her, simply because we had different skin colours. It was a concept foreign to her, having never experienced it in her lifetime.

"My God, Mum, that was so awful. I appreciate the effort, but you really didn't need to try so hard."

"It was always a touchy subject with you, ever since you were little." My mum's immediate deflection, a clear indication of how her feelings hadn't changed when it came to the subject of racial sensitivity.

"I know that's how you felt," I said, "but both you and Dad were a big part of the problem."

All this talk of the past had finally raised the issue that would be a tad more complicated to deal with. I wish my dad hadn't been so busy upstairs, because if we were going to end up talking about it, there were definitely things I wanted him to hear.

As I grew older, I became painfully aware of certain views my parents held when it came to specific demographics of people. Views that I found more than a little unsettling. My mum, in particular, seemed to show real prejudices towards people of colour. In the beginning, I didn't understand it, so I chose to ignore it until I couldn't.

With their views, I often wondered why my parents would choose to adopt outside of their race. Was it a conscious decision? Or did they just want to adopt regardless of what children they ended up with?

As an adult, I learned the term "white saviour," a term used to refer to white people who feel that their superiority obligates them to help or "save" people of colour because those communities lack either the resources or intelligence to help themselves. As horrible as it sounded, I felt it was the most appropriate term to use when explaining my mum and dad's unique parenting initiatives. My mother, in particular, had a strange sense of "saving" my sister and me from ourselves.

To me, she demonstrated a certain naiveté which hindered her ability to see the world around her objectively. That, coupled with her stereotyped perceptions of people of colour, formed an ignorant narrative of the struggles of people different from her.

I remember being told, "You're not 'black-black,'" or "We don't consider you like them..." when making the distinction between us and other black people. The difference being that we were being raised *her* way, the true way, the white way.

The reasons behind my mum's prejudices were complicated. Context matters and so does intention, and I had always been clear that her beliefs didn't come from a place of hate, but from a place of ignorance. Each of my parents displayed their own unique brand of problematic behaviours, but when it came to my mum, her notion that our culture and identity were somewhat irrelevant was ridiculous. Nonetheless, because of her beliefs, although born of misinformation, she genuinely thought that she could save us from what she considered to be our inescapable plight.

Despite her good intentions, some of my mother's attitudes became even more evident as I got older, resulting in many conflicts between us.

With my mum, there was definitely a lack of understanding as to why my culture and heritage were important to me. After all, she was raising me, so why would I need those things? It was difficult to explain to her that when we left home, we weren't seen by others through her eyes. I couldn't just enter a room announcing, "At ease everybody, my parents are white."

In the outside world, people's prejudices often made them see my colour first, and sometimes nothing else. One could say that in some ways, my sister and I were being done a real disservice, as we couldn't possibly be expected to grow into the strong resilient people of colour that our society would require us to be.

Of course I know that my parents did the best they could with what they had, and what they knew, and just because they were misguided doesn't mean that they weren't well-meaning. Growing up in Glasgow, Scotland, during the Second World War, my mum was a product of her environment, which was affected by poverty and a lack of education. She was part of a generation whose prejudicial views would prove extremely difficult to shift. To be fair, she didn't have many interactions with people of colour, and the ones with which she did weren't exactly the finest examples of people in general. My dad's first wife, who was black, was continually in and out of their daughter's life, so it gave my mum a little exposure to her family.

The only black man my mum had really known was the brother of my dad's first wife, who married a white woman, and whose infidelity was unparalleled. So, when it came to how she viewed black people, especially black men, there was no question about how she felt. In fact, my mum was convinced that all black men were the same. She even went so far as to say how disappointed she'd be if my little sister dated someone black. "They don't treat their women right" was her justification. It seemed a strange reaction. After all, what did she see when she looked at me? Just because my white parents were raising me didn't mean I would grow up and suddenly change colour. I was still going to be a black man, and it would have no bearing on how I treated a woman, or anyone else for that matter. Inevitably, my sister chose to date white guys, but I was never really sure if her decision was influenced by our mum. For me, it was easier to date people that I felt would have shared life experiences, and I just didn't think a white person would be able to relate. I dated only one girl from junior high through high school, and she was of African descent. She was my first true love, and with her, I felt my first real sense of belonging at a confusing time in my life that had me feeling too black to be white, and too white to be black.

Because I'd always been an openly proud person of colour, my mother's opinions only fuelled my mistrust of white people. We would argue about the views she held, and quite often, extremely hurtful comments were traded back and forth causing me to resent her.

Staring down into its contents, I started to realize that this box was becoming a real nuisance. It was stirring up old shit that I thought I'd let go of years ago, and was now suddenly made to relive reluctantly and without warning.

"Hey Mum!" I yelled towards the kitchen, as I'd noticed she'd returned there to refill her empty glass. "Do you remember that big social studies project I had in grade eight?"

"Are you kidding? How in the hell could I possibly be expected to remember some school project you had over thirty years ago?"

"Oh, you know the one," I argued. "I chose to write about the Underground Railroad, and the effect it had on modern-day black Canadians, and you said that 'slavery was a long time ago, and that people shouldn't focus on that.'"

My mum sat down again, becoming noticeably irritated at being forced to remember that confrontation from so many years ago, but I needed her to know how upsetting it had been for me, and how from that moment on, my impression of her had changed drastically.

I'd remembered phrases dropped into her rant such as, "Black people walk around with a constant chip on their shoulder," and "They need to get over it." And while stunned by what she'd said, I managed a retort: "The Second World War was a long time ago. Maybe we should tell everyone who lived through that to just get over it?"

My mum was enraged. "That's completely different," she shouted. "My town was bombed in the war, and it wasn't that long ago."

There had clearly been a double standard there. Feelings seemed only valid if they affected her or people like her.

That argument had taken place so long ago, but I remembered it so vividly because it forced me to see a side of my mother I didn't want to admit was there. Now, she was sitting right in front of me, and to be honest, I felt a bit shitty for having brought up the subject.

"I don't want you to think that I truly believe that," she asserted. "If I could take it back, I would, but what's done, is done." I could see in her eyes how horrible she felt, and it seemed cruel to continue to dwell on it.

"I know," I said as I threw some more items from the box onto the "don't keep" pile.

With my mum, I'd learned to try as best as I could to steer clear of topics that involved race, or anything of a political nature, thereby avoiding any conflict. It proved to be extremely difficult, and as a result, I wasn't always great at holding back my feelings.

Although my parents shared some similar views, I had more confrontations with my mum, possibly because I just didn't see my dad as often. Once again, in the 70s and 80s so many fathers took on the role of breadwinner, and the task of childrearing fell mostly on mothers. Because of this, I was ultimately left to deal solely with my mum most of the time.

Being born and raised in Canada, my dad was decidedly more liberal, although he too was a product of his environment. There were behaviours that he displayed that were also problematic, although different from those of my mum.

Though no Adonis, he carried himself with that kind of confidence. He was average looking with chestnut hair and a bit of a beer belly. As a small child, I think I saw him as a much larger man than he was, although he was only five foot seven. His glasses sat very high on his nose, and wrapped themselves tightly around his thick sideburns and over his ears. They were a fairly strong prescription, but in no way hid my dad's piercing blue eyes that would pop out of his head whenever he'd get angry, which seemed often.

He liked to think of himself as progressive and open-minded because he'd married a fourteen-year-old black girl in the 1950s, when in Canada, it was illegal to do so. That is to say, her being black was illegal, not the being fourteen part. This was something he would proudly assert to anyone who'd listen. My feeling was that marrying his first wife had more to do with his objectification of women, and his fetishization of black women in particular.

Between my parents, the relationship with my dad was the most complicated. With my mum, at least I felt I knew where I stood, and what her beliefs were, regardless of whether I agreed with her. Having spent so little time with him, I lacked insight into what my dad was really like. Because he didn't have much time to spend with his children, it was difficult to crack that outer shell and get to the meat of who he was.

If I had to guess, I'd have to say my dad's favourite past-time was sex. The truth of the matter was that he loved women, and considered himself a man of unabashed sexual pulchritude.

The wicker rack in the bathroom proudly displayed a collection of my father's adult magazines, the majority of which featured black women. It would be hard to imagine my mother not being offended by this, especially since she couldn't possibly make herself any whiter if she'd sat in a tub of Clorox. She seemed to tolerate my father's behaviour as I suppose most women did with their husbands in those days, even though it must have been difficult for her.

My parents, or at least my dad, loved to party, and he looked for any excuse to throw one even with the kids in the house. The biggest of the year was during Canada's Grey Cup, which was confusing to me, since nobody in our house watched sports of any kind, let alone football.

Our household, like many others of the era, had a basement family room complete with wood panelling and a floral-patterned chesterfield. The room was dimly lit except around the main focal point, which was of course, the bar. During many of my parents' gatherings, I would alternate with my sister at playing DJ and serving drinks. Mostly beer and the odd glass of Black Tower or Blue Nun, nothing too hard since I was only about eight or nine years old at the time.

Music blared from the wall-mounted speakers, and the air was thick with cigarette smoke. This, combined with the asbestos floor tiles, created an image that could have been pulled straight from a modern-day Surgeon General's warning ad.

Photography has always been a popular way of documenting the human condition, and the pictures taken at my parents' parties provided a treasure trove of evidence into the goings-on in our household. As an adult, I looked at the old photos through a much different pair of mature and experienced eyes, and although I'd been uneasy about what I'd discovered, I could hardly say I was surprised. There were the usual shots of my parents' friends, Auntie this, and Uncle that, and they were usually with someone else's significant other. They'd be kissing and groping each other while nobody seemed to mind.

Looking back, I didn't really know what to make of my parents' parties. I always had suspicions that there were some things of a more salacious nature happening once the kids went to bed, but in order to prevent more emotional scars than I could handle, I chose not to investigate any further. Suffice it to say, my parents were very sociable, and as a result, I was introduced to many people of varying backgrounds.

I'd always argued that the only people who really understand the true dynamic of a couple's relationship are the people in it, and so I'd always resisted opining on whether my parents loved each other. My interest was solely in my relationship with each of them as individuals. I will admit that in my adult years, learning about what my father referred to as his "indiscretions" was disturbing to say the least, and made me realize that however he felt, he would inevitably have to find a way to reconcile his past.

When it came to him as a parent, for the most part he was firm but fair, although when pushed, he had difficulty controlling his temper. He was no longer the 125 pounds of snarlin' death that my mum described him as in his 20s. He was much bigger now, with a lot more muscle mass. He could be extremely kind, but there were many times when I pushed him to a point where he became a little heavy handed. I'd never known my dad to have been raised any differently, and he himself never offered any insight, so I can only assume that he parented in the same way his father did.

In the early 1980s at the age of twelve, while attending one of my sister's ringette games, I was involved in an altercation with some older boys at the arena. In an attempt to lessen my feelings of weakness, I directed my anger and frustration toward my little sister as I began hitting her and pushing her around. That moment, when the bullied became the bully was met with the ire of my father who wasted no time in handling the situation. He was furious and who could blame him. He hauled off and punched me in the face. Hard. Immediately I could tell by the look in his eyes that he was filled with agonizing regret. There was more than one lesson learned here. Lashing out in anger is never the answer, and it sucked to be on the receiving end when someone loses control. My dad took it a step further when he decided to take that opportunity to teach me how a man defends himself. He wanted me to show him that I had what it took, but he gave up when it was clear I wasn't up to the task. I had never seen my dad that angry before and it left me feeling somewhat unredeemable.

It wasn't unusual for kids my age to get hit. Quite often, I would get smacked or clipped in the ear for doing something stupid, but my father reserved the belt for the big stuff. What I called my "high crimes and misdemeanours." The belt was a form of punishment that both my sister and I had come to know quite well, and my dad was always the one to give it.

As far back as I could remember, it was his job to bend us over and make us drop our pants so we could take a few lashes across the backside with that long strap of worn-out leather. If we'd committed any acts that were belt worthy, he'd yell out his trademarked expression, "Get upstairs and bare your ass," at which point we'd head immediately to our rooms and assume the position.

Now you'd think that I would have learned to just keep quiet and take my punishment like a man, but as I'd already come up short in that department, I took it the only way I knew how; kicking, screaming, and running around trying to avoid getting hit. My efforts though were futile as he would simply wait for me to pass while he landed blows where he could.

My mum never got physical with me, but she could definitely give a good tongue lashing. Her and I would argue terribly, and those situations would often result in a routine "wait till your father gets home" moment. There was no denying that I had substantial trauma which manifested the intense anger that I could neither understand nor control. As a result, those confrontations with my mum could be horrible, and the things I said were often regrettable.

At one point, my dad was so fed up hearing about my arguments with my mum that I was not allowed in the house when he wasn't home. He would head to work around six o'clock in the morning, so I'd be woken up just before he'd leave. I was expected to be out of the house while he was gone, and since I didn't have anywhere to go before school started, I was put out in the backyard with a pillow and blanket like a dog being put out for the night. Of course being autumn in Canada, that one quilt wouldn't have kept me warm if I'd set it on fire.

After school, once again, I was expected to wait outside in the yard until my father came home which was about six o'clock in the evening. Once inside, I was allowed to eat dinner with the family, but then straight to my room afterwards. This went on for weeks until I was deemed no longer a problem for my mum.

That whole situation only fueled my anger toward my parents, because at the time, I felt they went out of their way to hurt me. As a result, I was constantly pushing back and challenging their authority because I genuinely felt that I couldn't love them.

When it came to confrontations, weekends were always the worst. I'd be stuck at home with no means of escape, and even if I could, I had nowhere to go. Arguments would ensue, and though they would start out based on something as small as my complaining about having to take out the garbage, they would always spiral into full-blown shouting matches.

Often, I would head to my room where I'd slam the door and purposefully crank up my music to a decibel level high enough to ensure that my anger and frustration were felt. I understood this would enrage my father, who in turn would burst into my room and quite literally make sure I felt *his* anger and frustration.

It was difficult for me to find ways to have an emotional release, and once that pressure became too much, I would lash out at things around me. Punching a wall or smashing in the screen door felt satisfying at the time, but such reactions were definitely not healthy ways of handling situations.

Because of my inexplicable destructive behaviour, my dad would understandably lose his temper. Even if his intention was to simply talk to me, I would find ways of pushing him to his breaking point. It's no wonder that sometimes he ended up hitting me. He probably felt he had no other choice. I was stubborn and defiant to the point that I didn't care what my dad would do, so long as I found a way to hurt him back.

My sister later relayed to me how much it hurt her to listen to those beatings. She wanted me to just shut my mouth so that things wouldn't get worse, and honestly, there were times when I wish I had. But my pain was so deeply rooted that I don't think I was capable of stopping.

In a desperate attempt to help me, my parents agreed to send me to a psychiatrist. Unbeknownst to me, it hadn't been the first time they'd tried professional help. Inadvertently, I discovered my parents had fed me Ritalin when I was quite small as a way to control what was perceived to be hyperactivity. I'm not sure if they put it in my food, or simply added it to my bedtime vitamin regimen between the cod liver oil and the Flintstones chewable vitamin, but they obviously thought something was wrong with me, otherwise, why medicate me without my knowledge?

Working with the psychiatrist made things a little easier, although I know my dad wasn't really buying what they were selling. It wasn't that he didn't believe in problems with mental health, he just thought that with me, they'd missed the mark.

My sessions with the doctor did have some impact on me, and I started to get a better understanding of my feelings. Being able to address some of the trauma of my past was a difficult process, but it did turn out to be helpful. The arguments with my mum and dad began to subside, but there were still problems bubbling near the surface.

I developed some coping techniques that allowed me to "control my emotions," a phrase my mother had written out and taped to the front door for me to read every morning before I left for school. In hindsight, the reminder should've been taped to the outside of the door so I could read it before going into the house. It might have saved me from a few unnecessary altercations which would predictably end with the release of my uncontrolled rage.

It also felt good to be able to talk to the psychiatrist about my grief over the loss of my identity. That increasing separation from my ethnicity was something that I would continually learn to deal with well into my adult years.

4

I GUESS THIS IS GOODBYE

"Oh my God, you have one of my high school graduation photos! I don't even have one of these."

"Of course we do," my mum said. "We had it in a frame with your sister's, but since it had that stamp across it, we replaced it when you gave us one of your headshots."

I couldn't afford to buy my graduation photos, and the proofs that I kept had the photographer's watermark across them. When I gave them to my parents, I didn't anticipate that they'd keep any, since our relationship had been so strained at the time.

To be honest, how I managed to graduate at all was a bit of a marvel because of the difficulties I had in both my junior and senior years. Neither of my parents would have been aware of what I'd endured then, and I'm not altogether sure that they'd ever be prepared to hear about the specifics.

The high school I attended was a little more diverse than my previous schools, probably because there were many more students from around the area, and most of those neighbourhoods started to look different by the mid-1980s. Once again, I gravitated towards the black students and made friends with a few in my grade. Because there were only a handful of us, it wasn't that hard to do.

I was having minimal drama at home and was doing just as well in my classes as I'd done in junior high. In my spare time, I kept up with my musical interests, and still enjoyed my comic books and sci-fi novels. In fact, the only real issues I had in my freshman year were with my unapologetic fashion choices.

I had developed my own unique sense of style, and although I'd been making somewhat of a fashion statement, it was one that screamed: "DIFFERENT." Foolishly, I was under the impression that my clothes and my unique interests wouldn't matter within such a large student body, but as anyone who's ever attended high school in North America knows, those things matter immensely. Sir David Attenborough would most likely describe the average North American high school as being comprised of very distinct social groups which needed to co-exist within a self-contained civilization, and depending on how you identified, this determined your class in its society. To be honest, I originally didn't feel the need to belong to any of the cliques within the confines of those classroom walls, and as a result, I became the target for some of the bigger ones.

I took pride in being my own person, unique, and probably a bit odd and unconventional. I still wore glasses, although my round wire frames were somehow cooler than they'd been years earlier. Keeping up with the times, I used a generous amount of Dep gel in my hair every morning to ensure that not even gale-force winds would blow a single strand out of place. I was still a bit overweight, but I like to think I wore it well, even though my clothes were often considered weird and old fashioned.

Dress shirts and ties were something I wore often, and there would regularly be a pair of suspenders thrown in to complete the overall look. Sometimes I'd mix it up with a bowtie, and if I couldn't find one that matched my ensemble perfectly, then I would make one.

Actually, I sewed a lot of my own clothes, which was an inexpensive option to some of the more overpriced items you'd find at the mall. I became known as the goofy kid in the bowtie and suspenders, which initially I didn't mind because I didn't fully understand how the social order worked.

For a lot of kids to feel accepted, they would instinctively pick on others who seemed different. It was a classic misdirection, meant to pull focus away from themselves, who might have otherwise been labelled different as well. Ultimately, those acts of either attacking or excluding others probably gave the cliques and those in them a feeling of strength and unity, but at the expense of the poor target, which in this case, happened to be me.

I did my best to ignore the destructive criticism from some of the other students, and instead focused on my schoolwork. It was important to me that my grades were good enough to ensure a decent post-secondary education.

Initially, I had only been subjected to comments about my appearance and over-achieving personality. However, things changed when it became clear I was interested in music and theatre. When word got out that I'd been cast in the school musical, *Bye Bye Birdie,* I was instantly labelled as one of "those guys," which opened me up to a whole new world of ridicule.

The few friends that I had would always come to my defence, and it was comforting to know that someone had my back. As people of colour, we found it best to stick together because we knew that there would be strength in numbers. My circle made me feel a little less like an outsider, even though in reality, we were all outsiders.

My performance in *Birdie* went over pretty well, and soon I was looked on as being fairly talented by high school standards. It was a lucky break for me, because a student who was seen as a standout within their designated social group, commanded a certain level of respect from the others, much like a political leader at a world summit.

I managed to get through my freshman year fairly unscathed, and although my self-esteem could have used a boost in the end, it wasn't a bad start. Honestly, as far as the level of bullying went, it could have been much worse.

In my sophomore year, however, things sort of went to shit. My sister had started her freshman year, and because she was a friendly and outgoing student with supermodel looks, she became instantly popular. Not just with people in her year, but with students in all grades. She had actually started modelling professionally, as well as playing pretty much every sport offered at school. I found myself playing second fiddle to my younger sister who was smarter, better looking, and definitely more interesting than I could ever hope to be. Upon hearing my last name, it wasn't unusual for other students to ask if I was related to her, to which I would always respond, "Yeah, I'm her brother. I've been going to this school for over a year!"

My insecurities started to push my anxiety and anger to the forefront, and I started feeling completely unseen, not just at school, but at home as well. My sister was always off in some sort of sports tournament, or her agent was sending her off on photo shoots for magazine ads, while I had nothing interesting going on at all. I was invisible. There was no school musical that year, which meant I didn't have any real outlet except band practice, which only led to an annual trip to Canada's Wonderland.

Without anything to focus on, I found my emotions running high, especially when I thought about my parents' perceptions of me. There began a sort of paranoia that went along with my insecurities, and as a result, I found myself feeling ostensibly unimportant.

My sister excelled at everything, and in my eyes, that meant she was my parents' favourite. For years I'd always believed I was jealous, and the guilt that I had from feeling that way was overwhelming. Although jealousy was certainly part of it, I'd always been extremely proud of her, so I knew there had to be more to it.

Eventually, I was able to admit to myself that I had been afraid. Not that my sister would outshine me, but that she would eventually outgrow me. For the longest time, it had been her and me against the world, and no matter what, we had each other. Now she was popular and making so many new friends that I started to feel forgotten.

Conflicts with my parents became more and more heated and I started to spiral into a depression. On more than one occasion I ran away thinking I'd never go back, although inevitably, I always did. When I'd return, of course the fighting would continue, and even though I could handle myself fairly well in an argument, I was no match for my dad's temper.

Feeling that I had nothing remarkable going on in my life, I became lost and overcome with a sense of worthlessness that left me feeling I had no way out.

At the end of her freshman year, my sister was invited to the senior prom. On that night while she was out, I ended up in another unpleasant situation with my mother. As it escalated, I lost control of myself and began to smash things around the house, and my mum became so frightened that she felt she needed to leave. After she'd gone, I was left alone in the house. Alone, afraid, and feeling anger and shame at my inability to control myself. There was never a time that I *meant* to be destructive, but so often I was too overwhelmed by my feelings that I couldn't fight the urge to lash out. Waves of sadness washed over me and the darkness of where I found myself seemed so inviting that I simply didn't want to exist.

My father kept a gun in his bedside table, and though I tried desperately to open the box it was kept in, without the key, it was impossible. Instead, I went into the garage where I found the tank of gasoline for the lawnmower, and the matches for the barbeque. I knew that this way wouldn't be pretty, and it would most assuredly be painful, but nonetheless, it would be effective.

It's difficult to remember a lot of what happened after that, because by then I had become so detached from reality. What I do remember vividly, however, was a profound sense of sadness, and pain, followed by a feeling of numbness, as if there were nothing to see or hear around me. My sister and her friends had returned to find me just before I'd gone up in flames, and I was rushed by ambulance to the ER of the local hospital. There, I remained silently lost in my own head, numb to a world that seemed to be closing in around me.

At the time, I figured my parents were somewhat apathetic to my situation, but I hadn't realized how traumatized they were over the whole thing. At the hospital, when the on-call psychiatrist suggested that there was nothing wrong with me, and that I should just be taken home, my dad completely lost it. He knew that I was suffering some sort of mental health crisis, and demanded that they find a way to help me. In the end, I remained confined to the psych ward for two whole weeks.

When I returned home, my parents and I never really talked about what had happened. I tried to assure them that I'd be able to control myself, but we never really addressed it other than that. What I wanted was a fresh start, but understandably my parents found it difficult to trust me after what I'd put them through.

Even after my failed suicide attempt I still had difficulty emotionally. I would never be able to move forward with a clean slate because the damage had already been done. Arguments with my mother became more frequent, and proportionately, so did the number of confrontations with my dad. I was intransigent when it came to my beliefs, and I would use any means necessary to get my point across.

Things came to a head one evening when at the height of an argument I challenged my father, asking if hitting me made him feel like a man, which only triggered him to become angrier. Once again, I was pushing him to his breaking point, so I should have known what would happen next. He'd cornered me by the front door of our house, and in his enraged state, he bashed my head into the wall so hard that the brass embossed plaque with the prayer "Bless This House" ironically fell from where it had been mounted. Why was I so angry? And why did I feel the need to hurt my parents? I wouldn't fully understand until I was an adult, but in those moments, I could only guess that I'd been taking my anger out on those closest to me, without ever thinking that they'd eventually reach their limit. After that altercation, I ran away again, only this time, my parents decided that it would be best that I don't return. I felt fine with their decision because I knew deep down inside that it was what I really wanted as well.

It's said you should be careful what you wish for, because you'll need to be prepared for how to handle it should it come true. I certainly wasn't prepared. I was just alone, with nowhere to go, and no one to turn to for help.

5

THE MUSIC AND THE MIRROR

It was 1987, and I was a sixteen-year-old kid in high school. But unlike most of the other kids my age who were struggling with homework and midterm exams, I was on my own afraid and struggling to survive. I had little means to take care of myself. In fact, apart from a few changes of clothes and my schoolbag, I had little of anything at all. I was homeless, alone and becoming more anxious and desperate by the minute.

With the permission of his mother, one of my good friends allowed me to stay on his sofa for about a week as I ardently continued to look for something permanent. My efforts were fruitless, however, and out of options, I found myself spending some nights on the street.

Having exhausted my search for somewhere to stay, and with nowhere else to go, I ended up in a local men's shelter. It was meant to be a temporary solution, but it took some time for social services to step in and help me with the financial resources I needed for suitable accommodations. It was a waiting game I had no other choice but to play.

The shelter was set up as one large open space, consisting of beds that were separated by flimsy curtains, similar to the ones you'd find in a shared hospital room. I was provided a little place to put my clothes, and a cot with blankets and a pillow. For the most part, it was comfortable, but I never really felt safe. There were men in the shelter, with varying sets of circumstances, but I was by far the youngest person there. I was basically a child left feeling abandoned and more than just a little afraid. As best as I could, I tried to keep my head down in order to avoid any strange or unpleasant interactions.

Meals were given every day, and I would try to wrap something up to take with me to school for lunch. Sure, I continued to attend school, but the lack of a support system coupled with my living conditions made it very difficult to focus on much of anything. Trying as best I could, I still managed to squeak out half-decent grades, which somewhat surprisingly was still important to me.

Time seemed to move at a deliberately sluggish pace in the shelter. I had difficulty sleeping while being consumed with nightmares of what might happen to me if I couldn't find a permanent place to live. Youth Assistance, or Student Welfare, was available to kids sixteen and over, so I just had to wait for my application to be processed. I explained to my assigned social worker how desperate I was to find anywhere to live, and that I would take any place as long as it got me out of the shelter. But it didn't help. Things seemed to take forever, and I was reaching the point of wanting to run from where I was and never look back.

My makeshift room was definitely not an appropriate place for a sixteen-year-old. The fabric used as "walls" lacked both the dimensions and thread count needed to keep out prying eyes, particularly those of one male facilitator who would make a habit of visiting me late at night. He was someone I met when I first arrived at the shelter, and he seemed very sincere and eager to help. There was a kindness to him that I'd never seen in a stranger before, and it seemed that whenever I struggled to figure things out, he was always there to lend a hand. It was like I had someone watching out for me, and I felt safe knowing he was around.

He would often stop and talk to me. Nothing special, just casual conversation in passing. But his questions eventually became more personal in nature, and that's when it got a little awkward. He wanted to know about the kind of girls I was interested in, and what, if anything, I had done sexually. It seemed really weird at the time, but as a kid who was eager to please, I tried to answer honestly.

At night, he would come to where I slept, and he would show me adult magazines. It's strange that the thing I remembered the most was how different the girls looked from the magazines my dad had displayed in the bathroom.

The first time he put his hands down the front of my underwear, and touched me, I didn't know what to do. I froze. All I could do was look straight down at the pictures and try not to make eye contact while he touched himself. The one time I did look up, I noticed him biting his lip, presumably to stop himself from making any noise. I can still remember that weird smile he had, the kind that showed more of his gums than teeth. There was a part of me that was afraid, although I was never really sure why. Was I afraid of him? Or was I afraid of disappointing him in some way and he'd end up not liking me anymore?

I always felt so dirty when he left. It was a shameful guilty feeling, and for the longest time I thought there was something wrong with me because I knew that it was wrong, but said nothing. There was part of me too, that liked the attention. When he was around, I felt special, and not so alone. When he'd leave, he would reassure me that my stay in the shelter was temporary, and that things would get better for me. I wasn't sure if he was suggesting he'd be able to help speed up the process somehow, but I think I believed that he could.

My fear notwithstanding, he was able to convince me that he was my friend, and I believed him. Maybe if I just let him do this, he'll get me out of here, I thought. I'm not even sure I understood what was really going on. I just tried to block out everything around me, while I prayed for him to finish up and leave. Eventually, when so much time had passed, with no indication I'd be leaving the shelter any time soon, I started to clue in that he was more than likely full of shit. He continued to make his "random bed checks," and I was helpless to do anything.

When I finally got approved for government assistance, I found a permanent place that was willing to accept applicants in my situation. It was a sort of boarding house, and although it wasn't perfect, I had my own room, and it was only a short bus ride to school. Most importantly, I was finally able to get out of the shelter, and leave behind the shame of what happened to me there.

The room that I rented was in the basement of an old town house. It had a shared kitchen and bathroom, as well as shared laundry facilities with the house next door. There were two middle-aged men occupying the other rooms, and separating us all was a small kitchen with only enough room for a stove and sink. Each bedroom had its own fridge, so I was able to keep my food separate and in my own space.

I barely left my room, which meant I had limited exposure to the tragically depressing odour of the common areas which I determined to be a combination of stale beer, mac and cheese and a hint of desperation.

I had mixed feelings about my situation. The first night in my room, which had little more than a desk and a chair, I sat on the edge of the little single bed, and cried. How had I come to be in this situation? My new living accommodations were a far cry from what I was used to in my parents' middle-class, four-bedroom house, and yet I felt a sense of relief that I was on my own.

With my newfound independence, I did things the way I wanted without fear of retribution, so on my first trip to the grocery store, I filled my cart with items I'd only dreamed of eating. With so much focus on my weight growing up, I was never allowed to have sugary breakfast cereals. Since the time we were small children, my mum only offered my sister and me three choices: plain Cheerios, Rice Crispies, or Corn Flakes. All options were boring enough, but to add insult to injury, a scoop of bran was mixed into whatever we chose, making us the most regular kids at school. In a sheer act of defiance, the first meal I had on my own consisted of several bowls of Count Chocula. the cereal I had always wanted my mother to buy, only to be denied it repeatedly. It was the ultimate "fuck you" moment, knowing how angry it would have made her knowing that I was eating such garbage.

Even though I had my freedom, I was uncomfortably nervous about my new accommodations. Because of what happened at the shelter, I avoided any interaction with the strange men living in such close proximity. For several weeks, I only showered or used the kitchen at night when everyone was asleep, minimizing the chances I'd run into anyone.

They were very difficult times for sure, but despite my living conditions, I tried to keep up with my schoolwork. I knew that focusing on academia was the key to getting myself out of a temporary situation that could easily become permanent. I had never felt more abandoned than I did at that time, and yet I became determined to make something of myself. Fuelled mostly by anger, I made it my mission to do well, despite those who had left me behind.

Socially, I was still finding my way as I dealt with the pressures of having somewhere to belong. As teens, we often shifted social groups depending on where we felt we fit in from year to year, and because I admired their status in school, that year I tried my luck with the "preppies." This was arguably the hardest group to keep up with simply for the financial implications alone.

Regardless, I chose to seek out membership despite my obvious disadvantage. I was flat broke. Unfortunately for me, what preppies valued most was their aesthetic, which carried a hefty price tag. To be a "prep" required money, and lots of it. Ralph Lauren Polo button-down shirt: $100. Bass brand Weejuns-style penny loafers: $130. Levi's 501 jeans: $50. Being part of a group whose existence was the very definition of privilege: Priceless.

In a moment of unbridled enthusiasm, and naïveté, I actually thought I could get away with some department-store knockoffs. I bought a couple of generic button-down dress shirts without the little horse guy, along with some department-store-brand penny loafers, that I felt were similar, and hard to distinguish from, the real thing.

In the wild, my deceptions may have gone unnoticed, but if confronted by a preppy in captivity, I would be subjected to a higher level of scrutiny. Although the look I'd pulled together wasn't half bad, to a true follower, I was simply nothing more than a poser.

I was laughed at behind my back, and sometimes right to my face by other students who I thought were friends, and I came to realize that I simply didn't belong. So, leaving most of those people behind, I went rogue and decided to rebrand. There was no way I could have kept up that look financially, anyway. I frequented a few used clothing stores and was able to throw together a look that required minimal effort. Black turtlenecks and jeans were simple enough and didn't draw a lot of attention, which was exactly what I was now looking to avoid.

Very few people knew my living situation. Only a few close friends from my music class and band were in the loop, though I generally didn't like to talk about it. At the start of one of my early morning music classes, I'd been having a conversation with a very good friend. I was telling her about my new living arrangements, and more specifically, how I wasn't able to get a telephone where I was living. I'd been in contact with the phone company, but my request for a line was met with a fair amount of resistance because of my age and (lack of a) credit history. For people in that situation, their policy demanded a $250 deposit. The government must have felt that having a common form of communication was a bit too extravagant for the underprivileged, because there was no provision for it in my assistance. I was going to have to accept the fact that I wouldn't have access to a home phone.

At the end of the class, my music teacher pulled me aside to ask how I was doing. He must have overheard my earlier conversation because he offered me the money for the deposit on my phone. Having never known such kindness from someone I hardly knew, I was overcome with emotion and couldn't help but throw my arms out and hug him tightly. In that moment, I imagined myself being able to one day share that type of moment with my own father, but with all my pain and anger, I knew that it would be a long time coming, if ever.

Once I had a new phone installed, things became a little easier. Keeping up with the bill that came with it however, was challenging. In fact, I found it quite difficult to manage a lot of my expenses. My welfare check could only stretch so far, and even though money was never spent frivolously, there was little to nothing left at the end of each month after paying for rent and utilities. It was overwhelming, to be honest, and at times it was even difficult to put food on the table, let alone pack a lunch.

There were days when I missed school altogether because being hungry would have made it too difficult to concentrate. On one particularly hunger-filled afternoon between third and fourth periods, I decided to borrow fifty cents from someone for the vending machine. I thought that at least with a candy bar or bag of chips I would be able to make it to the end of the day. After delicately inserting each quarter and scanning each row of snacks for the treat with the best value for money, I finally landed on the honeybun. I could feel myself start to salivate in anticipation, but in my hunger-induced light-headed state, I must have pressed the wrong letters on the keypad. Not realizing my mistake, I reached into the bottom of the machine to claim the sticky sweet pastry, only to find a pack of spearmint gum. Not just any spearmint gum, but the '80s type of stick gum, lightly dusted and so stale that it snapped in half when you opened it. The feeling of absolute defeat didn't stop me from making the best of a bad situation, so one by one, I ate each and every stick in that pack. I chewed and swallowed as if each bite were part of a savoury four-course meal.

Running out of food was a normal occurrence. This, combined with my regular dance classes as well as my daily bike rides to and from school, brought about considerable weight loss. I'd slimmed down to a shadow of my former self, which didn't go unnoticed by the other students at school. Most people attributed it to a recent growth spurt, since I'd also grown a few inches that year.

Returning from school and having to think about creating yet another meal out of mostly condiments was like a constant punch in the gut – until the day I arrived home to find several bags of groceries outside my door. There was everything I could have hoped for, and with a lot of non-perishables, I assumed that they'd come from a food bank. I wasn't sure if it was part of something provided by social services, or how they'd have known that I was in need. Not wanting to look gift food in the mouth, I decided not to question it further, and simply accepted the food drops which continued for several months.

Years later, I heard that my friend from high school music class had lost her father. As I was relating my condolences, she told me that her father had been the one who'd left the groceries at my door. She said that he had always seen something special in me and thought that I just needed a little help to succeed. All those years and I never knew. I wasn't very good at holding back my emotion, but I didn't care. Once again, people other than my parents were able to give me a helping hand, leaving me resentful and feeling that the relationship with my parents had been fractured beyond repair.

With the stress of hunger momentarily lifted, I was not as clouded and unfocused as I'd been. But because of late nights at work, I was still tired, and even though I would show up to class, I was having difficulty. I'd picked up a part-time job as a fry cook at a fast-food restaurant in the hope of getting a little more monthly income to work with. Sadly, what was then called a student minimum wage ($3.85 an hour), forced me to work ridiculous hours in order to make even the slightest bit of difference. Honestly, the money wasn't worth the effort, so I decided to look for a job that would allow me to take home a little more cash, and fewer grease burns.

A few years earlier, I had been a volunteer at a local hospital where I had developed a very good reputation. So, when I heard that they were looking to fill a part-time position in their chronic-care facility, I jumped at the opportunity.

"Did you ever think I would end up working in healthcare?"

My mum, still in her chair across from me, suddenly perked up, leaned forward, and didn't hesitate to answer.

"Well actually, now that you mention it, I did. I expected you to follow through with school, and become a nurse like you were supposed to."

The look on my mum's face showed that she was still less than impressed at the fact that I'd chosen not to finish nursing school, and with so much time having gone by, I realized that I'd probably never hear the end of it.

In my junior year of high school, I accepted the part-time position at the hospital, which was by far the greatest part-time job I'd ever had. I was what was known as a feeder, and my job was to do just that - help feed patients who were unable to feed themselves. Being able to help people was extremely rewarding, and it made me rethink my possibilities for the future.

After working there for a few months, I knew I really wanted to continue helping people, and so, I decided to pursue nursing as a career. I was hoping that my parents would be thrilled that I'd chosen to do something that would provide a steady income. And although I thought it would put us on a path to reconciliation, a path that at the time I felt was my responsibility, I wasn't doing it for them, I was doing it for me.

Having this new goal in mind, I set out to meet the criteria that would allow me to be accepted into the college program after high school. It would require me to keep my grades up and maintain a certain average in order to be considered, but making ends meet was also a priority. I would also need to make time for some music and dance, because that was an extremely important emotional outlet for me. All things combined meant I truly had my work cut out for me.

Keeping up with my dance classes gave me a strong sense of self-confidence, and it was in class with my teacher from Theatre Aquarius that I felt most at home and safe. I was never a great dancer, probably because I started later than most. I knew I was never going to dance with the National Ballet or anything, but when it came to my jazz and contemporary classes, I could definitely hold my own.

In the beginning, I thought that my dance teacher hated me because he had a no bullshit approach to his teaching. And he wasn't shy about using profanity-laced critiques during rehearsal, often singling me out in front of the class. Despite that, he pushed me to work harder than I had ever worked before, and I grew to understand that being tough was his way of getting the best out of me. He saw something in me that I don't think even my parents had seen, and he took the time to nurture it. As a mentor, he made sure that I had the support I needed to succeed.

The confidence I'd built there gave me the courage to audition for a high school musical. It was part of a regional showcase which was done every year with students from Hamilton and the surrounding area. The show would rehearse a few nights a week after school, and would run for a few weeks at the end of the year.

That year's production was *Anything Goes,* a musical farce from the 1930s with music by the great Cole Porter. The story is set on an ocean liner headed for New York City, and I was cast in the small role of one of two "Chinese converts." Although I was ashamed of how I chose to play the part, I desperately wanted the opportunity to be in a big musical. I guess for that time, I fell in line with the status quo and saw nothing wrong with the racist caricatures that were often written into shows of that era.

I was disappointed to see that there were only three other people of colour in the show, one of which was my onstage counterpart. Although he was actually Chinese, it stood out to me that he was offering a similar stereotyped portrayal of his character. It seemed like we felt the need to give audiences what they were expecting, and not taking into consideration how it made us look or feel.

Despite the racial composition of the cast, I was suddenly part of a select group of people who all knew each other from past shows, and I made some deep connections to some wonderful people who became good friends.

My love for theatre and acting began to grow, and by the time *Anything Goes* finished its run, I'd been bitten by the acting bug. I liked being able to become a different person onstage, and what's more, I was good at it. The door was now open, and I decided to take a big step and walk through it.

The next show I did with the high school musical showcase was another production of *Bye Bye Birdie,* and it was being performed in the studio theatre of Hamilton Place where I'd attended summer theatre school. It was a building that was starting to become so familiar that it often felt like a second home.

I was making friends with kids from several schools in the area and this was expanding my view of the world as I was introduced to people from all different walks of life. A lot of the cast had appeared in the previous year's show, so I was comfortable in a sea of familiar faces, but I also enjoyed getting to know the new ones.

I had a small ensemble role, with a solo in the very first scene. I worked hard and did the best job that I could as I became more comfortable singing. In fact, I was finding my own voice. It was a big change from accompanying myself with a guitar and singing folk songs, and I found it both challenging and enjoyable at the same time.

My abilities didn't go unnoticed, and subsequently, the director offered me a paid job in his summer theatre company *New Faces*. I didn't hesitate to accept, and even though it didn't pay a lot of money, it was more than I'd been making at my hospital job, and it would give me the chance to perform, which was something I'd have done for free.

When we finished our last performance of *Bye Bye Birdie,* I was invited to my very first cast party. I'd never had so much fun, and for a brief moment I was able to forget about my problems, and just enjoy the company of friends. I felt that I finally had a place to fit in, and I was becoming a happier person because of it.

With a newfound self-esteem, I felt I could reach out and try and have some sort of relationship with my parents. Initially, it was difficult because of the anger I still felt towards them. But despite knowing that it would take a long time for my emotional scars to heal, I decided to give it a try.

We started out with phone conversations and progressed to visits at their house. I think we were all on our best behaviour for a month or two, and I was desperate to keep any conflict at bay. Theatre had given me an emotional outlet in which to focus and control my feelings but because we didn't address any of the issues that had landed me where I was, it didn't take long for us to end up back in the same loop we'd been in so many times before.

I made the mistake of expressing to my mum my excitement at being a part of an Afro-Canadian Association that had been started by some students at McMaster University. As if time had stood still, she started to become defensive. It wasn't enough that she didn't understand why I would want to be part of that group, she made a point of asking why I was so focused on it. According to her, I only ever spoke about my blackness, and never about being anything else. Personally, I didn't know any mixed-race person, who when asked, would identify themselves as part white. White people often use that line of questioning with people that have an ambiguously ethnic look in an attempt to understand why they *aren't* white. And so, the dance continued. My mother and I would go around in circles and I'd grow increasingly angry and frustrated trying to make her understand my thoughts and feelings.

Because I'd spent so much time in theatre, my grades had slipped a bit, and my mum was worried that I wouldn't be accepted to nursing school. She was genuinely concerned that I might fail and as a result, lose out on an opportunity for a good life with a good paying job. I was trying to focus on my studies, but music and theatre had been bringing so much light into my otherwise dark existence that I didn't want to let them go.

Over time, I became irritated at the thought of my parents' having certain expectations of me, and considering I didn't even live under their roof anymore, I felt they had no right to dictate to me how I should live my life. At least now I had my own place to go home to, and thus, was able to walk away from the situation and stay in control of my emotions. But in order to protect my feelings, I distanced myself from them again.

I continued doing what I had become used to, which was to keep up with my dance classes, and theatre, while making sure I got passing grades. It had become difficult financially, even with a part-time job, and try as I did, I was rarely able to pay for my dance classes on time, if at all. Fortunately, my dance teacher, who'd been aware of my situation, always welcomed me to class regardless of my financial status.

At the end of my junior year, I was approached by my dance teacher about the Theatre Aquarius summer school senior program. This program was for older students and would take up the bulk of the summer. They were doing a production of *A Chorus Line* at the end of the course, and since there were very few male dancers that year, he was hoping I would attend. Once again, I had difficulty paying for the tuition, but because my teacher was the principal, my lack of payment somehow went unnoticed, perhaps accidentally on purpose.

A Chorus Line is set on a bare stage, and is centred around seventeen dancers auditioning for chorus roles in a Broadway musical. I played the role of Paul, which was quite challenging for me both as a dancer and actor. Not only did the character need to be one of the better dancers, but his monologue is a heart-wrenching coming out story known by most everyone in the theatre world. I felt a real connection to the character since I knew then that I was attracted to both men and women, something that was rarely discussed openly at that time in the eighties. Even in my own family there were insensitive comments made about gay people. Mostly by my brother-in-law, who's disdain for "queers" pretty much cemented my choice to never discuss the subject as it pertained to me. As a person of colour growing up around a large number of small-minded people, I wasn't prepared to add to the list of things that would make me a target. I'd always admired the courage it took to come out at a time where people weren't as accepting, especially at the height of the AIDS crisis, which added so much stigma to an already extremely marginalized group of people. When portraying Paul, I drew from my own thoughts and feelings about my sexuality, and the anxiety I felt trying to hide it. In the end, I think it helped me in coming to terms with who I was.

My focus was split rehearsing *A Chorus Line* in the mornings, and then later in the afternoon, rehearsing a show for *New Faces*. But I managed. There was no denying that I was spread a little thin, but I was happier than I had been in years.

Just prior to our first performance of *A Chorus Line,* my grandmother passed away and as upset as I was, I chose not to attend the funeral. I'd been so blinded by my anger towards my mum, that instead, I went to a technical rehearsal that lasted all day and into the evening, feeling that it was more important.

"You know, Mum, I don't think I ever told you how sorry I was that I didn't go to Gram's funeral." I could feel a lump of sadness in my throat as I confessed this to her.

"What are you talking about?"

"I always felt terrible about not going. You'd lost your mother, and I should have realized then that it was about so much more than just being there for her, it was about being there for you."

"What are you on about? I wouldn't worry about it."

This was not the response I'd expected from my mum, and honestly, I felt a little ridiculous tearing up at that moment, only to have her brush it off as if it were nothing.

"Oh, okay, I just wanted to let you know that I'd been bothered by that for years."

I truly did regret having not been there for her, regardless of how I was feeling about our personal relationship, but since she hadn't given it too much thought, I figured I could finally let it go.

When I first left home I was fairly certain most people, including my parents, assumed I would end up the subject of a tragic story on the local six o'clock news, but I was starting to show that I had potential. The performance I gave in *A Chorus Line* was reviewed positively by the *Hamilton Spectator*, and because they were also impressed with me in the *New Faces* shows, all the feelings of self-doubt I'd had for so many years were silently slipping away.

My parents never saw any of those productions, and honestly, it was sad to think that if they had, they may have looked at me differently. I poured my heart and soul into every moment onstage, and because my emotions came from a very real place, they might have been able to catch a glimpse of the real me.

In the same clichéd way many professional actors recall their early beginnings, I too will confess that I was chosen to play Jesus in a production of *Godspell* in my senior year of high school. It was a lot of pressure, and although I tried to keep my focus, I could feel the stress of being pulled in so many directions affecting me. There was no way I was going to give it up though, because that production of *Godspell* was more than just a show to me. It was a statement. I was a person of colour in a lead role, which was something that didn't happen very often. The show became my number one priority, and although I knew my grades weren't as good as they could have been, I figured I'd find a way to get by.

Godspell earned me many positive reviews, and as word spread about my performance, through newspaper articles and interviews, my parents agreed to come see the show. I was convinced that seeing my talent, and the attention it garnered, compelled them to view me in a different light. My perception of how my parents showed affection was distorted by the resentment I had for them and the feeling that they were to blame for my living situation.

I was getting a bit of a name for myself within the small local theatre community and with all the acclamatory reactions for my performance, I continued to associate my talent with my value as a person. At the time, watching my parents so excited at the praise being showered on me made me feel they were erroneously taking credit for my accomplishments. I wasn't emotionally mature enough to understand that they were genuinely happy to see me thriving. Instead, I was disappointed that I would be seen as being successful because of my parents rather than being successful *despite* them.

Once again, I was offered a job with *New Faces* for the subsequent summer, which I accepted with the intention of saving money for the next year's tuition. I had been accepted into a college nursing program, and with a good post-secondary education came the potential to lift myself out of poverty. For once, things seemed to be falling into place as I looked forward to one more summer of theatre before heading off to college.

It wasn't until after I'd committed to *New Faces*, as well as Theatre Aquarius's summer production of *Hair*, that I realized I was missing a chemistry credit which was a prerequisite for the nursing program. Without it, I wouldn't be able to start college in the fall, so I would need to take the course in summer school. I should have declined doing one or even both productions, but instead, I decided to go all in. The decision to try and do everything all but guaranteed a frenzied, yet exciting summer. In the end, I gave well-received performances in *Hair*, as well as with the *New Faces* musical revue – all the while managing to pull off a fairly decent grade in chemistry.

As the summer drew to a close, I began to prepare for my upcoming year at college, something I'd been anxiously anticipating since graduation. Nursing was an excellent career, and something I felt I'd be extremely good at, but as I tried to focus and make it my top priority, I couldn't stop thinking about the stage. It made me feel special. A feeling I'd always longed for. Certain I'd be incapable of managing both my nursing schoolwork and theatre, I knew I needed to make a high-stakes decision, but was terrified I'd make the wrong one.

My parents were firm believers that getting an education, and a steady job, were the key to one's success, and since my relationship with them was slowly moving in the right direction, I didn't want to upset or disappoint them. On the other hand, I had a passion for performing, and would always wonder if I had what it took to do it professionally. After some serious soul searching, I finally chose to take the road less travelled and drop out of college to pursue acting. The odds were certainly stacked against me, but I felt it was something that I needed to do.

I'm fairly certain that my parents were not pleased with my decision, but who were they anyway? I was still feeling like they'd abandoned me at a point in my life when I was very vulnerable, and left me to fend for myself. It was because of them that I'd been homeless, and it was because of them that I ended up being targeted by that predator in the shelter. I was definitely not going to let them influence how I chose to live my life.

My mum gave me a huge lecture about needing a steady job with benefits and a pension like my dad. She drilled into me the importance of saving money and eventually buying my own home. Things, she pointed out, that being a so-called actor would make near impossible to attain.

Her patronizing tone enraged me, and what I said to her next surprised even myself. I asked her if she wanted me to end up like my father, because I certainly didn't want to. I may have in fact said that it would be worst thing I could do. My heart sank deep into a painfully intense regret as I realized what I'd just said. I knew I didn't really feel that way. I simply said it to hurt her. My mum became very quiet, and instead of arguing with me, as I most certainly thought she would, she simply ended the conversation then and there. We didn't speak for quite some time after that.

When the reality of what I'd decided to undertake finally set in, I became overwhelmed with sadness and fear. No job, and no prospects, I was lost, and almost immediately began to regret my rather hasty decision to pursue what was now beginning to look like a reckless flight of fancy. Perhaps I hadn't really thought things through, but I had no other choice but to quietly panic as I tried to figure out how to move forward despite feeling so unrehearsed.

6

I HOPE I GET IT

If I'd learned anything from the television drama *Fame,* it's that New York was where anything could happen, so I began to search out anyone I knew who had a connection there.

Before long, I was in contact with a drama teacher that I'd known from his involvement in community theatre. He had a former student that had moved to New York a year earlier, in 1989, and was studying at an acting studio there. We'd never met, but after talking on the phone, he was kind enough to invite me to stay with him to see if I liked the city.

Strapped for cash, I scrounged up enough for a Greyhound bus ticket, and although I was eighteen and had barely been outside the Greater Toronto Area, I left Hamilton and headed to New York to prove myself. I had stuffed my clothes in an old canvas mail bag that had been used to store an old tent, and though it was somewhat cumbersome and heavy, I managed to get it to the bus station. Cramming it into the undercarriage of the bus, I boarded and eagerly scanned the rows for an empty seat. Who would have guessed that there could be so many different yet equally horrible smells in one place? It was going to be a twelve-hour drive, so I chose to find a way to keep both my head and my lunch down as I pulled my baseball cap over my eyes, and my shirt up over my nose.

The atmosphere in the cabin suggested that I was on my way to a convention of the ill-mannered, as more than a few people travelling that day seemed to have their voice controls set to loud and unfiltered. Wanting to avoid any unpleasant encounters, I decided it was best to feign sleep the entire trip.

Having put little to no thought into what I was doing, I used the duration of the excruciating bus ride to come up with a plan. It wasn't just about finding a way to break into the business, I was going to need a contingency plan in case everything went to shit. I figured I would try and find a regular job while I auditioned for anything and everything that I could. It began to feel like I'd put all my eggs in one basket in a do-or-die career move, but I was in New York City, the epicentre of theatre. If I was going to try to make it, I might as well go big.

Giving myself two years in New York to find myself some kind of work as an actor felt like a reasonable amount of time. After that, I could re-evaluate my situation and decide whether to stay or go back home to nursing school. In my mind, it seemed as good a plan as any and a way for me to say that at least I'd tried and failed, rather than never having tried at all.

Arriving at Port Authority late in the evening was exciting. I could feel how truly magical the city was, and I immediately understood its allure. There were so many sights and smells, although none as horrible as what I'd been inhaling for the past twelve hours. What struck me almost immediately was the number of people out so late at night. I'd never seen anything like it. I'd been used to the stillness of Hamilton's city streets after around ten o'clock during the week, but New York was buzzing as if it were the middle of the day on a weekend.

Of course I expected to see signs for Broadway shows, which were everywhere and they did not disappoint. *Cats, Once on This*

Island, Phantom of the Opera, Les Misérables, they were all there. All larger than life. And when I finally made it to Times Square, what I didn't expect to see was the vast number of advertisements selling something else New York was famous for at the time, which was sex. The city has changed so much since, but what I got to see was some of its seedy underbelly, up close and personal. With adult cinemas, and strip clubs with live sex shows, it was the New York I'd seen on television and in movies, and as happy as I was to see it cleaned up years later, I still had a sense of nostalgia when it came to the Times Square I'd been first introduced to. It provided me with some of my most interesting life experiences, as I was quite young, and not ashamed to say that occasionally, curiosity got the better of me.

When I met my new friend, he introduced me to his roommate. They shared a small studio apartment that had a couple of futons in the centre of the room where they would sleep. Honestly, it reminded me of my room at the boarding house, only this was considered almost luxury by New York standards. We stayed up to talk for a while, but my friend and his roommate had school in the morning, so we kept it fairly short, although the excitement of being somewhere new, combined with the sounds of sirens going off constantly, kept me awake most of the night.

At breakfast, I was shown a few points of interest on a map of the city, but I was left to discover things on my own for most of the day. I had always been told to be careful in New York, especially riding the subway, and on my second or third outing, as I rode Line 2, I found out why the hard way. From West 96th to Times Square seemed a fairly easy route to take, and I felt I had a handle on how the subway worked. I even got used to the way the cars were so crowded, and how the people were practically standing on each other.

Admittedly a slave to the fashion trends of the '80s, I unabashedly wore the infamous fanny pack. Where else could I have efficiently stored my essentials in one convenient and easily accessible place. As we arrived at the 72nd Street platform, I was shoved from behind, and felt a tug on the strap around my waist. When I turned to look, the doors were closing, and I felt someone pushing past me as they tried to make off with my stylish yet functional fashion accessory. The assailant had tried to cut the bag off, but was thwarted by their own inability to keep a sharpened blade. I looked around to see who had tried to rob me, but as the subway doors finally closed, there was just a sea of people exiting the platform.

Checking myself out, I noticed a small cut on the strap of my pack that hadn't gone all the way through and a small dot of blood on my shirt where the tip of the knife must have poked me while it was slipped under the strap. It left only the tiniest of puncture wounds, but the way I recounted the story of being stabbed on the New York City subway guaranteed me a little street cred. Undaunted, I wandered around Times Square completely captivated by the sights and sounds which were almost overwhelming. Everywhere I turned delivered a flash of sensory overload. From the neon signs to the tumult of the street traffic, I felt as though I was being swallowed by the city itself.

Now, looking up at my mum, I realized that there were so many things about me that she didn't know, just as there were things I never knew about her life before my sister and I came along.

At that time, neither of my parents really knew who I was and who I was becoming because we simply never talked about anything important. I would love to have shared with them how it felt to move all the way to New York, or how exciting it was to attend an audition for a big Broadway show. Regarding some of the more questionable things I'd done, that wouldn't have been in the cards. I'm not sure my mother would have been able to look me in the eye as I recounted some of my recreational activities. If she'd found out about my addiction to pills and alcohol, would she have thought less of me? Would the respect I'd gained over the years simply disappear? One thing was for certain, I would never learn the answers to any of those questions. There may be some things that parents and their children just aren't supposed to know about each other, although if they did, it might help loosen the wedge that sometimes comes between them.

I don't think I knew what the hell I expected to happen when I arrived in New York at such a young age. It may have been sheer stupidity or just that I was so monumentally naive that I thought I could just show up and start an acting career. At least as a U.S. citizen, I was able to find other work in order to support myself while I looked for ways to break into the business.

I landed a part-time job at a Lower Manhattan restaurant that gave me enough income to eventually move to a new place with a new roommate. If I wasn't at work, I'd be leafing through *Backstage* magazine looking for auditions, while never losing the determination to find success in spite of those who I felt didn't believe in me. As a busboy and barback at the restaurant, the tips were minimal, but I had most of the days free for possible auditions, and even in the evenings when I worked, the city came alive and I was able to meet people of all different backgrounds.

The Broadway Dance Center was where I took dance class, as did so many other aspiring hopefuls looking for their big break. It was one of the first dance schools to offer drop-in classes with several different genres, and dancers working the front desk from time to time were allowed to take some classes for free, so I took full advantage.

There were always open call theatre auditions that allowed both union and non-union actors to attend, and I managed to be seen for a few. There was a summer stock production of *Hair,* as well as a cattle-call for *Cats,* both of which proved to be extremely rigorous. The auditions themselves were exciting, but the anticipation of the desired outcome felt almost euphoric.

Cats held their auditions at the Winter Garden Theater, and because I'd been fascinated with the show from the moment I saw it in Toronto years earlier, I just knew I needed to go. Standing on the actual stage where the singers and dancers performed the show each night was not only inspiring, but humbling as well. Quite ironically, the exaggerated scale of the set mirrored how small I felt in such a huge city.

All of us nervous hopefuls were separated into groups, and when mine was called, we were lined up across the stage. The choreographer went down the line and immediately cut about half the dancers. It turns out, they were looking for a few specific roles, which meant there were height requirements. Even though the decision wasn't based on ability, getting past the first cut literally made me feel a bit bigger than I had when I first arrived.

The remaining dancers were taught part of a combination from the show. I managed to pick it up pretty quickly, and when we danced individually, I gave it everything I could. It paid off, and I was asked to come back later to sing for the creative team. I was so nervous that I went for a walk to calm my nerves before going back in to sing. After I'd finished, I was thanked for coming in, but I never heard from them again. I was in no way disappointed because I'd had such a great time auditioning. Going in with zero expectations, and getting farther than I anticipated, was a success in my book.

Expecting to stay in New York for at least a full two years, I was beginning to get settled into my new home. With a job and an apartment, I was off to a good start, and had only positive things to disclose to friends back home. When reporting back to my old dance teacher and mentor in Hamilton, he unexpectedly asked if I would be interested in going home for a couple of months. Theatre Aquarius was moving out of the studio theatre of Hamilton Place and opening its own brand-new theatre complex in the heart of the city. They'd been looking for some local talent to be in the theatre's opening production of *Man of La Mancha*, which he would be choreographing. Since I hadn't been able to book anything in New York, and it seemed to be a short enough engagement, I jumped at the chance for a paid gig. I was good on my rent, so I knew I'd be okay for a couple of months. And heading back to New York with a professional credit on my resumé would definitely be an asset.

The new complex had an eight hundred seat state-of-the-art theatre, and would be a huge boost to the community. My mentor who had known me and my work so well, recommended me to the artistic director, and so I was cast in the show. It was thrilling to know that I'd be a part of such an exciting endeavour, especially with a theatre company that I'd had such a connection to.

The journey back home was difficult. Not the trip itself, since this time I'd upgraded from the bus to a train, but because I would potentially have to face things that I felt I'd been running away from. Almost everything about being back in Hamilton brought back shitty memories to be quite frank, but I was determined to make the best of the situation. I would be gainfully employed as an actor for the first time, so that was something at least.

During rehearsals, I stayed with a friend from high school who was attending McMaster University. She was living with her mother and sister in their home not far from downtown Hamilton, and they were kind enough to offer me a spare room. Once again, I was being helped by people I barely knew, and I couldn't have been more grateful for their kindness.

Man of La Mancha had me working with some amazingly talented people, and though it was difficult for me not to be nervous, I did my best not to look too much like a fish out of water. The cast was rounded out with professionals from all over Toronto, so I was a little unsure as to what I'd be contributing to an already stellar group. Ultimately, because he knew my abilities, I decided to trust the choreographer's professional opinion, and not consider myself to be just a last-minute diversity hire.

The show required a musician who could also be onstage as part of the ensemble, so my guitar skills were one reason I'd been hired. I didn't actually play flamenco guitar, and although I'd overexaggerated some of the skills on my resumé, I knew that wasn't one of them. I did manage to get the basics down in order to play what I needed to, and even to my surprise, I did pretty well. All in all, rehearsals were going great, until all of a sudden, they weren't.

In a fairly simple scene where I was portraying a prisoner being dragged from a cell to an interrogation, the director wanted me to appear without any clothing. I hadn't anticipated being pulled out of a trap door and out of my comfort zone so early on in my career, but there I was in a kind of limbo, not knowing how I was supposed react. I was not at all comfortable with what was being asked, especially since I'd heard that the director had taken a bit of a liking to me. I assumed I was cast in the show because he appreciated my talent, however his request made me re-evaluate what I was really bringing to the table.

At eighteen, and just starting out, I didn't want to appear difficult to work with, so I said nothing. Fortunately, the costume designer, sensing my discomfort, managed to convince the director to put me in a small loin cloth, which was basically a dance belt with a piece of burlap hot-glued to it.

In those days actors were often made to feel that if we wanted the gig, we would do what we were told, so ultimately, we had little input when it came to some of the design decisions. I wore the loin cloth, and didn't say a word about it, although the insecurities I had about my body left me feeling somewhat disgusted with myself after each performance.

Regardless of the costume design, which up to that point, had been the most public of my many humiliations, the show was a huge success, and it was even more impressive because of the new theatre we had just opened. It was an honour to be one of the first people to perform on that stage, and to be a part of something so especially unique.

I never contacted my parents to let them know about *Man of La Mancha*. I was convinced that they wouldn't see what I was doing as a route to a viable career, so I wanted to make sure I had more than a small ensemble role in a local theatre production in order to prove to them that I could make something of myself. This job should have been an opportunity to show them that I had potential but stupidly, my anger and pride held me back from sharing it with them.

7

RAINBOW HIGH

I was still sifting through a ton of old newspaper clippings when I came across an article from the *Hamilton Spectator* about the opening of *La Mancha,* and the building of the theatre. It was stained a bit yellowish but was completely smooth without a trace of creasing. The article took up almost the entire front page of the entertainment section, and it featured a still from the show. It was a great photo of the cast, and I was excited to see that I was actually in it.

I gently skimmed through the article, and started to feel a little sentimental.

"I wish I'd invited you guys to the Theatre Aquarius opening. *La Mancha* was such a great show, you would have loved it."

"I understand," my mum said, and left it at that. I think she'd felt a similar regret about the state of our relationship then, and the fact that it prevented me from sharing my professional debut was something she really didn't want to dwell on.

When *La Mancha* ended and I prepared to return to New York and continue what I'd started, I contemplated my next steps on my theatrical journey. Surprisingly, I was once again approached by my mentor, this time suggesting that I consider getting myself an agent. He had an excellent relationship with a Toronto agency that represented his children, who were working actors in television and film and had been part of some fairly high-profile projects.

It was certainly an interesting and exciting development. An agent would help get my foot in the door, but I hadn't really given much thought to the Toronto musical theatre scene which was just starting to proliferate. Only a few big shows had opened there since *Cats* at the Elgin Theatre in 1985. *Phantom of the Opera* and *Les Misérables* were the most recent shows to open Toronto productions featuring Canadian casts in 1989.

Figuring I had nothing to lose, I decided to give it a shot, and at least meet with the agency. The worst that could happen was they wouldn't be interested, but if I got lucky, I could hold off on going back to my five square feet of luxury in New York, as well as cleaning tables and hauling cases of empties for tips.

Toronto had always excited me. In high school, I would often ditch class with a friend and take the bus there, just to hang out. We'd hit the record stores, and shop for cheap knockoff designer clothing and accessories. It's where I bought my first "Rollex" watch, and underestimating my classmate's spelling competency, I anticipated being able to pass it off as the real thing.

Taking the bus to the city was easy enough, and because I'd known the general downtown area, I was able to walk to the agency in a few short minutes. My sister had supportively given me one of her old portfolio cases she'd once used for modelling, and I filled it with pictures and reviews of performances I'd been in. Other than that, I really didn't have very much, so I was anxious to hear what they'd have to say.

When I arrived at the address off Yonge Street, north of the financial district, I discovered a two-level building with retail stores on the bottom and businesses on the top. I found the entrance and walked up the small narrow staircase that led to the second-floor. When entering the office, it felt fairly unassuming for a well-known talent agency comprised of three partner agents and their associates. Meeting with the most senior partner, I was understandably a bit nervous, but I'd been assured that all the agents there were pretty down-to-earth, so I kept that in the back of my mind as I sat down to chat. The conversation was straightforward, and when the agent spoke to what they could do for me, I was a little caught off guard. I thought I'd be put through more of a job-type interview. I'd never really considered that the agency would be working for *me*, which made me feel weirdly important somehow.

Without really explaining why, the agency decided to represent me. Perhaps it was because they saw me as a survivor, something I'd grow to realize was an important characteristic needed in order to make it in the business. I'd had my personal struggles, and when the odds were stacked against me, I was still able to make a name for myself, even if it was in the small local theatre community of Hamilton. Whatever the reason, I knew that my mentor was partly responsible, so I had to make sure I didn't disappoint him.

Instead of heading back to New York, I gave notice to my roommate there, and found an apartment in Hamilton to sublet from a friend of a friend. I was anxious to see how things would be with an agent, and if they could actually help me find work in the industry.

My first professional headshots were taken by one of Toronto's most sought-after photographers at the time, and I was nervous because of how I felt about my appearance. He was patient and made me feel extremely comfortable as he sat with his camera in one hand, and kept the other free to sip his coffee and smoke a cigarette. His conversation was engaging, and he spoke on a number of topics with confidence. Every so often, he'd put up the camera and snap a picture. This candid approach is how he managed to capture images that truly represented who you were.

With headshots and resumés, I was ready to start auditioning but had concerns about finding my way around. I'd been used to getting into Toronto, but I wanted to get more familiar with the transit system inside the city.

"You know, Mum, you were the one who taught me how to get around in Toronto. The street names were so complicated, not like the numbered ones in New York. Who knows where I could have ended up."

My mum would often tell me which subway line to get on, and which stop to get off at, and, "If you ever get lost," she said, "look for the CN Tower and you'll know you're facing south." It was sound advice that I passed on to my own daughters when they were old enough to start exploring the city on their own.

She knew a lot about Toronto, and we used to go there quite often. Usually we'd have dinner and see a show, something my parents both really seemed to enjoy. Smiling to myself, I reminded my mum of the dinner we had when we'd gone to see *Cats* for the very first time.

"You know, my girls didn't believe that you stabbed me with a fork," I said to her. "They thought I made the whole thing up." I held back the urge to laugh, because when I looked at her face, she appeared to be unamused.

On a special occasion like a show in Toronto, my mum's favourite place to eat was Ed's Warehouse. Owned by Honest Ed Mirvish himself, there were several restaurants that were separate from each other but all located on the same block. The options were endless. Seafood, Chinese, roast beef, you name it, whatever you were craving, you could get it at Ed's. It wasn't fine dining, it was more like having a homestyle meal surrounded by kitschy interior décor. Needless to say, my parents thought they were getting a taste of class – at rock-bottom prices.

I remembered the night of the fork-incident vividly. While in the middle of our entrées, my mum asked me to pass her the butter. Because I was engaged in conversation with my brother-in-law to the right of me, and thus didn't hear her, she had to ask again. When I didn't answer for a second time, my mum took her fork and stabbed me in the left shoulder with it, at which point she received my full and undivided attention.

"I told the girls that story when they were little, but they refused to believe that their Nana was capable of ever doing such a thing."

My mum laughed along with me but managed to pause just long enough to remind me with a deadpan look, "That'll teach ya!"

The agency was taking a huge risk, seeing that I had almost no professional experience to speak of. And I was uneasy with the fact that I hadn't booked anything after auditioning for a couple of months. I was sent out consistently for television commercial work, but since my previous experience had been onstage, I wasn't as comfortable in front of the camera. Looking back, it was crazy to think that because I hadn't booked any jobs in my first two months, the agency might drop me as a client, but it was something I worried about constantly since I was running out of the money I'd saved from *La Mancha*.

I was thrilled when I finally got a call about a theatre audition they had booked for me. It was definitely where I was most comfortable, and I thought that if I could land the job, not only would I not starve to death, but the agency might actually keep me on.

For the audition, I was asked to prepare two contrasting musical theatre pieces, which was easy enough. I had a lot of songs in my repertoire, but I thought it would be a good idea to know more about the show in order to choose something that would be appropriate. When I asked what the audition was for, they told me it was *Les Misérables*.

"Wait, what? Do they know what I look like?" I asked.

Their comically dry response was, "Well, they have your headshot, and they booked you a time." I still thought it was a bit unusual, having never seen a person of colour in any of the photos I'd seen of the show.

That said, I don't think I stopped practicing from the moment I knew I had the audition until the day of the actual audition itself. I was sure my neighbours in the apartment next door were getting fed up with having to hear me warbling for hours on end. They were such a nice couple and I didn't want to disturb them, but I felt that I needed the practice. I was already at a huge disadvantage being an actor of colour auditioning for what was arguably the whitest show playing in Toronto at the time. I tried my best to keep the volume down to a minimum, and I was happy that they never actually complained.

On audition day, I'd gone to the address I was given, but I thought perhaps they'd made a mistake. There didn't seem to be a rehearsal studio or anything like that in the area. It took me a bit, but it finally hit me. Wait a minute, I thought, this looks awfully familiar. I know this place. I was standing outside along the strip of restaurants owned by Les Misérables co-producer, Ed Mirvish. The very restaurants I'd eaten at with my family years earlier. It was a strange coincidence that I should be auditioning for a big musical at the same place I'd eaten at before actually seeing my first big musical.

With a newfound sense of confidence, I located a doorway, right between the steak and the seafood, and took the elevator up to the offices. The smell of fresh oven-baked bread floated up from the restaurant kitchens and through the building as I slowly made my way to the fourth floor. I entered a hallway, where several people sat waiting to be seen. I checked in and took a seat next to them.

The layout of the offices was such that it allowed me to hear other people singing for their auditions. This gave me cause for concern. What if I sucked, and all the other people auditioning could hear me? I wasn't sure I was ready just yet for that kind of humiliation.

I heard some pretty amazing voices while waiting my turn, and immediately thought to myself that I may have bitten off a little more than I could chew. If this is what they were looking for, I may have made a very big mistake. Suddenly, the smell of the fresh bread seemed slightly nauseating.

When they called my name, I made my way into the rehearsal room and was greeted by the resident director, the production stage manager, the musical director, and of course, the accompanist. When they asked what I had prepared to sing, out of sheer nervousness I launched into a whole spiel about a brand-new musical called *Miss Saigon*. Seemingly oblivious to the fact that the show was created by the same writers as *Les Misérables*, I went on and on about what it was all about, how it had just opened on Broadway, and the song I'd chosen to sing from it. Ugh! What can I say? I was eighteen years old…and nervous. Even though I'd had many auditions before, this one was particularly stressful because there was more than just a job at stake. I had worked hard and made huge sacrifices, but more importantly, I would be proving that as an actor of colour, I had something to offer.

Gingerly making my way over to the piano, and after discussing a tempo with the accompanist, I began to sing. At that very moment, my right leg decided it would involuntarily help me keep time. I don't think that the panel noticed, but I sure did. I found it extremely difficult to focus on my singing as I was distracted by my newly sentient and rather enthusiastic lower extremity. When my song was finished, I was thanked by the creative team and sent on my way. I was pretty sure I'd blown it.

The following day, after what I thought had been a complete disaster, the agency let me know that I was being called back. I indicated to them that I didn't do well, but they seemed unconvinced. My instructions this time were the same as before. "Prepare two contrasting musical pieces." At least I think the instructions were the same. To be honest, I wasn't paying that close attention because I was way too excited.

I practiced every song in my repertoire, and made sure to have at least nine or ten different songs for them to choose from. As long as they didn't ask for that song from *Miss Saigon*, I'd be okay. I wasn't about to take the chance that my leg would go off on another spasmodic solo.

I was completely ready on the day of my callback. It was raining, which was not usually a good omen, but I just smiled to myself as I got onto the office elevator. Inhaling deeply on my way to the fourth floor, the aroma of the bread baking in the restaurants below felt a little more comforting this time.

I checked in and took a seat, and as I waited patiently, wondering what they'd want to hear, I kept opening and closing my song book half expecting new songs to suddenly appear every time I did. Clearly, I was very nervous, and understandably so. A lot of work went into trying to find material that I felt would impress them, but one can never be too sure.

I was called into the rehearsal hall where I was met by everyone from my previous audition, but now with the addition of the associate director from New York. As I started to list off the songs that I'd prepared, the musical director raised his voice and said, "Now, just do exactly what you did the last time you were here." Oh no, I thought, not the *Miss Saigon* song. I took a deep breath, and with a significant amount of hesitation said, "Okay."

To my surprise, when I began to sing, both my legs decided to stay in their lanes and do what they did best, which was to ground me. I was able to focus completely on the song and when I'd finished, the musical director leaned back in his chair, looked at the associate director, and said... "There you go."

The associate director just stared at me from above his glasses, and then asked me to go over to the piano to learn a line from the show. It was from a scene that took place in the second act and was at the climax of the building of the barricade. The line ended on a high A, not an easy note, but on my first attempt, I nailed it. The creative team didn't say much other than thanks for coming in, which I took to mean thanks, but no thanks.

The following day, my agency called me with an offer to join the show as a member of the ensemble and an understudy for the role of Marius. As an understudy, I had to learn the role, and would be pulled out of my regular ensemble part to go on if the actor who played Marius couldn't perform for some reason. A lot of pressure, but exciting nonetheless.

I was in a state of disbelief to be honest. And I was finding it difficult to process what was happening to me. There was no way I could have anticipated how my life would change so drastically with a single phone call.

Out of everyone I wanted to tell, my parents were at the top of the list. After years of feeling as though I was a hopeless case, I was finally going to be able to prove to them that I wasn't a complete write-off. The relationship with my parents was strained after everything that happened when I was in high school, and I hadn't talked to them much since I'd been in Toronto. I really didn't want to have to explain to them the circumstances that ultimately led to my decision to move to New York. After all, I was still ashamed of the things I'd allowed to happen to me once I'd left home.

Their response to my news about *Les Misérables* was really not what I'd expected. It was as if the past had never happened. They wanted me to know that they always knew I'd find success, and even though it had been my wish to make them feel that they'd made a terrible mistake sending me off on my own, I accepted their validation of my choices. What happened? What was different now? Why were my parents acting as though our relationship wasn't arduous at best? Once again, I was convinced that it was my new-found success that gave my parents the permission they needed to show me any level of acceptance. In my world, success equalled love. Sadly, this misguided way of thinking kept me in a vicious cycle of being attracted to people who were both emotionally manipulative and physically abusive.

My sister used to call me the "prodigal son", which only made me further question my parents' motives. Once I'd landed that role in *Les Misérables,* it did seem as though they began to contact me more frequently, and with an acute sense of interest. Was it possible that my sister was right? Did she really feel that our parents' love for me seemed conditional? Undoubtedly, it was a simple joke that I regrettably took too much to heart.

On my first day of rehearsals, I went to the theatre to watch the show for the very first time. I'd told the creative team I'd seen the show, but in actuality, I hadn't. How could I? There was no way a kid like me would have been able to afford a ticket. So, I was both nervous and excited to be watching a show that I'd never seen before, and in which I, myself, would be onstage performing in just a few short weeks.

While walking down the street to the stage door of the theatre, grinning ear to ear in anticipation of meeting the cast, a pigeon suddenly swooped down in front of me, and shit right in my face. Although my whole life I'd heard that this was supposed to be good luck, all I could think was, Why me? Why now?

Making my way backstage, I went immediately to the bathroom. There, I managed to clean myself up and make myself presentable before meeting the cast for the first time. As I emerged from the bathroom, I bumped into my neighbour from the apartment next door to me in Hamilton. We both looked at each other in surprise, and I soon discovered he played keyboards for the show. I made sure to thank him for not getting upset with my practicing in the apartment, to which he admitted that when he and his wife heard me singing, they both thought that I would make a good addition to the show's ensemble.

After meeting most of the cast, I headed out into the house to sit and watch the show with the other new cast members. Once the overture began to play, I became somewhat emotional. My eyes welled up with tears as I sat there feeling a true sense of accomplishment. To think that just a couple of years earlier, I was barely making ends meet, and struggling to finish high school. Now, when all my classmates were worried about their university exams, I was in the cast of what was one of the most beloved musicals of all time.

There were two weeks of rehearsal before I went into the show, which I hadn't realized was not much time at all. If I was going to be ready, I needed to be super focused on that musical score which back then, ran over three hours. Since I absolutely loved every moment of what I was doing though, it didn't feel like as much work as it actually was.

As one of six replacements, there had been a fair amount of self-induced pressure for me to excel. And since as far as I'd known, up until that point there had never been an actor of colour anywhere in *Les Miz,* I felt I had something to prove. Pushing myself harder than I had ever done before, I set out to learn the show at break-neck speed, and once I'd finished learning the score on my own, I was ready for our first complete sing through with the full cast. Of course, I was super nervous to sing in front of everyone for the first time, so when the cast gathered in the rehearsal hall, I sat at the back of the room with most of the new recruits.

The musical director seemed happy with everything, as I held my own through the first act. It was mostly ensemble singing, so I was feeling pretty confident. However, when we got to the second act, I grew nervous about the upcoming solo I'd done at my audition. It ended on that high A, so if I was going to prove something to myself and the rest of the cast, I knew I had sing it perfectly.

When the time came and I prepared myself, I noticed that the entire cast had turned around from where they were sitting to look at me in anticipation of that big moment. As I stood there, I planted my feet firmly on the ground and nailed my line. The cast actually applauded, and the musical director put his pencil down and said, "Good boy."

What happened next was a true lesson in humility. A little later on in that sequence, not too long after my earlier shining moment, gun shots were meant to ring out over the barricade, and I had the line "Snipers!" Now the notes in the musical score had X's on them, but they were notes nonetheless. I was unfamiliar with the meaning of that symbol, and taking an extremely unfortunate guess, I interpreted it to mean that I could choose what notes to sing. Seeing as it had been such a crowd pleaser earlier, I figured I'd sing my whole line on that high A. So, I belted out "SNIPERS!!" and held onto the note, relishing in my own sound. The musical director politely stopped the rehearsal, looked at me and said, "You know that's just shouted." I was so embarrassed I could have died. The cast chuckled a bit as I sank down low into my chair, wanting to disappear. I learned that despite the old expression, sometimes you shouldn't try to end on a high note.

After that rehearsal, I felt more comfortable getting onstage with the cast for the first time. The six new cast members had a couple of onstage rehearsals with the understudies and swings before we actually had a full onstage run-through with the entire cast. It did feel a little weird to only have the six of us in full costume, but we needed to rehearse all our costume changes which for me, included several quick changes in the first fifteen minutes of the show.

The rehearsal went as well as I could have hoped, and being on that stage was a truly magical experience. At the time, I thought I'd never be a part of something so big again in my life.

At my first understudy performance as Marius, I was waiting onstage with the rest of the cast behind the curtain, waiting for the overture to start, when an announcement was made. It declared that I would be playing the role, and immediately there was an audible groan of disappointment from the audience, at which point a fellow cast member told me to have a good show. I laughed, knowing that he understood what it felt like going onstage as an understudy, and I continued on with the show. In spite of the audience's initial reaction, I took comfort in knowing that other cast members had my back.

I knew it would be difficult when I was ready to have my parents come to the show. I hadn't seen them in a while, and I wanted to make sure they knew I was thriving. Maybe once they saw the show, I'd get the reaction I'd been hoping for. Some small act of contrition over leaving me on my own at such a young age. The fact that I still felt this way was confusing to me. In my mind being homeless meant that my parents didn't love me enough, but my heart knew that they felt they had no other choice. Now that my life was finally on track, why couldn't I just let it go and move forward with the new relationship beginning to form between us?

I had been doing the show for a few months already yet there I was, extremely nervous knowing that they were in the audience and trying not to let it affect me too much. There seemed to be a few less disappointed sighs as they announced my name at this particular matinee performance, so things were already off to a good start.

I had a great show that afternoon, and by the time we got to the curtain call, and I was taking my bow, I managed to see my parents in their seats - or out of their seats rather, as I was stunned to see them up on their feet applauding with such enthusiasm.

After the performance, they came to meet me at the stage door and waited patiently as I spoke to fans of the show, and signed a few autographs. When I finally got to them, my mum threw her arms around me and told me how much she enjoyed the show. My dad hugged me as well, and told me I'd done a good job. We decided to go out to have dinner before they headed home to Hamilton, and at the end of the meal, when my dad asked for the check, he was surprised to find out that I had already taken care of it. It was extremely important to me that I showed them that not only was I happy with what I was doing, but that I was also able to take care of myself. Our relationship shifted after that day, and I think for the first time, I felt that I may have exceeded their expectations.

I'd reconnected with my family, and was now trying to make new friends in the company, which proved to be more difficult than I originally anticipated. I was extremely eager to please, and like with my parents, was desperate to find love and acceptance with this new group of people, even if it meant putting myself in situations where my behaviour demonstrated a lack of good judgement.

I began to hang out with a few cast members that liked to grab a drink after the show. It started out as the odd pint at the local pub down the street from the theatre, but it soon evolved. Eventually I found myself heading out to after-hours clubs where the nights often included not only alcohol, but cocaine and other drugs, which I did in desperation to keep up with the others.

Having dabbled with substances a bit when in New York, I sort of knew what I was getting into, but I wasn't used to it on such a regular basis and was often sick by the end of the night. Although I knew I shouldn't have been doing a lot of what I did, I really wanted to be liked. It was okay for a little while, but it got progressively harder to keep up. Cocaine was hard to come down from and I would often be left feeling exhausted. Things got so bad, that at one point when I returned home from a night of partying, I fell asleep on my couch with my clothes on and, my front door open. Not just unlocked, actually wide open. When I woke up a few hours later, I could barely open my eyes. I'm lucky nobody made their way into my place. God only knows what they could have done to me, although I was probably safe having pissed all over myself in my sleep.

On Sundays, I never really left my apartment because I needed the entire day just to recover. If I hadn't needed the odd trip to the bathroom, I would never have left my bed. This unhealthy routine left me feeling down. And when I thought of things that I'd been through in the past, I would end up in a very dark place. It didn't take long for me to realize that I was never going to be able to keep up with my new friends, and so, after months of late nights filled with reckless abandon, I decided that it was time to stop trying.

I still went out once and a while, but I would avoid smoking, and would nurse one beer all night, making it look like I'd had several. It was a lot of trouble to go to in order to fit in with a group of people that I hadn't known that long, so I pulled away slowly until the novelty wore off, and I started to limit my socializing after the show.

Although my experience in Les Misérables on the whole was a good one, there were a few disappointing elements that had left me feeling dumbfounded. It was clear that some of the cast had never worked with or even known a person of colour, and had difficulty figuring out how to act around me. I think this was what I'd tried to explain to my mum when I was younger. That in the real world, because of people's prejudices, I would be judged on my outward appearance almost immediately. I wasn't just seen as that guy; I was seen as that "black guy."

There were certain elements of casual conversation that were troublesome, and the constant microaggressions were quite revealing. There was a barrage of people's audition stories, about how they were up for a role, but they didn't get it because it had to go to a black actor, or how they couldn't be seen for something because they were white. It implied that they were losing opportunities to other actors simply because companies were trying to be more diverse. I always found that kind of shit offensive. These white actors were complaining to me, (someone of colour), that they felt it was unfair for them to be passed over because of how they looked. It seemed to me, a wasted opportunity for them to reflect and understand how it was for someone like me and so many other actors of diverse backgrounds throughout history who were completely limited in what we could audition for simply because of the colour of our skin.

During my time with the show, there had been a public outcry over the beating of Rodney King at the hands of police in Los Angeles. In 1992, at the end of the trial for the officers involved, the entire world was waiting to hear the outcome. When the verdict was delivered, and news of the officers' acquittal spread, it sparked outrage within the black community, causing riots and civil unrest, not just in Los Angeles, but throughout the U.S. and Canada as well. Toronto had its own protests against social injustice, which unfortunately led to what became known as the Yonge Street Riot.

Backstage during the performance that evening, as we learned of the violence and looting, I was asked by another cast member if I could run out and grab him some VCRs. To say I was shocked was an understatement. Who the fuck did this guy think he was? Was he seriously minimizing the complexity of this delicate issue of race relations? Did he look at the colour of my skin and assume I would be someone who would involve himself in lawlessness? At best, it was a joke that was in poor taste, but at worst, it was racism pure and simple.

Even though I was seething, I felt the need to swallow my anger and make it appear as though I wasn't bothered by what he'd said – or the fact that so many others had laughed along with him. What's sad is that these were people I admired. But after that, I found I couldn't look at them the same way.

My future seemed very unclear in that moment, and I wondered if I would have to deal with that type of behaviour everywhere I went. I also began to feel that I'd have difficulty finding roles where the colour of my skin wouldn't matter, even though the industry had just started a new trend of what they were then calling "non-traditional casting." Disheartened, but not dissuaded, I was still eager to get out there, and if I had to fight to prove myself, then so be it.

The show's run in Toronto was winding down, and even though there was a separate Canadian National Touring Production, our Toronto cast was heading out on a small tour for several weeks before closing the show completely. Travelling wasn't something I was used to, but a new adventure was a welcomed distraction from the mixed emotions I was having about the unpleasant experiences I'd had with some of the other cast members.

8

ON THE RIGHT TRACK

The call for me to join the Canadian National Tour of *Les Miz* came after the Toronto company closed in 1992. It was the same track I'd done before, and though it was a little strange to be doing the same show with different people, they were all great. I tried to keep my head down and keep a low profile since my experience in Toronto, but was surprised at the number of people who were so friendly and welcoming.

It made me realize that I didn't necessarily have to try so hard to be liked, or to make friends. In the past, I'd insert myself wherever I could in an effort to be noticed, which didn't always attract the most genuine of people. Here, I was learning that I could be quiet and more reserved, and yet still be noticed. I'm not sure if it was because we had cast members from the U.S., but I felt slightly more at ease with everyone. There definitely weren't any issues because of race, not even a joke in poor taste. I was seen as a peer, and for that I was extremely grateful.

We had Broadway veterans in the cast, including a Tony Award winner for his role in the show. Everyone was down-to-earth, and they really made me feel a part of the company.

Even with this different group of people, things still felt like business as usual, although this time I wasn't hanging out and trying to be part of the in-crowd. I decided instead to simply focus on the work, and my craft, always looking for ways to improve my performance. When it came to singing, I'd never had any formal vocal training, and so being able to rely on my natural voice made me fairly confident in that aspect. Where I decided to focus my energy was with an acting coach that could help me work on how to develop a character.

Revisiting the pain of my past traumatic experiences was something I'd grown to rely on in order to tap into the very real emotions I needed for a role, but it wasn't until this particular tour that I learned how much that technique could take its toll, especially when dealing with unresolved issues.

One evening, during a scene in act two, just prior to one of my solo lines, I felt a very strange sense of dread come over my whole body, and the feeling was terrifying. All the blood rushed from my extremities and I was overcome by the sudden urge to run away from the situation. Clearly, that wasn't an option, so I managed to pull myself together and sing. After the show, a friend in the ensemble approached me and asked if I was alright. She'd noticed a slight change in me during that moment, so I explained to her what had happened. She figured that I'd had a panic attack, and explained to me that she'd known a few actors who'd experienced them as well. I'd never thought something like that could happen to me onstage, in the middle of doing what I loved to do, but the use of my emotions from the past might have been having a detrimental effect on me.

Thank God I had someone in the cast I could rely on, and who understood what I was going through. My friend always made a point to find me onstage just before that same moment, and would either make eye contact, or touch my hand if she could, to let me know I wasn't alone. I always appreciated that she did that, because it made things a lot easier for the rest of the run of the show.

Before starting the tour, I had auditioned for the Toronto production of *Miss Saigon*, a show whose songs I was all too familiar with. It was the most recent of the "mega musicals," having its Canadian premiere at the brand-new Princess of Wales Theatre, down the street from where *Les Misérables* had been playing at the Royal Alexandra.

It was the highly anticipated new musical adaptation of *Madama Butterfly*, by Claude-Michel Schönberg and Alain Boublil that promised to be a stage-effects spectacular, complete with helicopter. Set in Vietnam during the weeks leading up to the fall of Saigon, the story revolves around Kim, a young bargirl who falls in love with an American marine named Chris. I landed a role in the ensemble, and not only was I thrilled to know that I'd have work after *Les Miz,* but the fact that it would be in a new theatre designed and built specifically for the show made it all the more exciting. I'd done the same in Hamilton for Theatre Aquarius so I knew the excitement of opening a new theatre, but being an original cast member of a huge Broadway show in Toronto would be a new and wonderfully remarkable experience.

The *Les Miz* tour returned to Toronto where it played for two months before finally coming to an end. It was during that time that I was called back in to audition for the full creative team of *Miss Saigon*. I was now being considered for one of the principal roles. Originally, I had been told by one of the executive producers that I wasn't suited for the role of Thuy, the cousin of Kim, and her betrothed. It was thought I was "too nice, like a marshmallow," and too far removed from what had been seen as more of a villainous character. I don't know why they changed their minds, but I was thankful for the opportunity to prove that despite having what they perceived to be a sweet disposition, I was a capable actor who could perhaps bring something new to the role.

When my name was called and I headed into the rehearsal hall for my final audition, I couldn't have been more overwhelmed. There were at least fifteen to twenty people at the audition table. The producers from London, New York, and Toronto were all there, along with the writers of the show, the casting directors, and all the creative team. Some I knew, but most I didn't, and I started to experience an uneasy but all too familiar feeling. My nerves were starting to take over, but I took in a deep breath, shook it off, and just sang the best high B flats I could muster at eight o'clock in the morning on a two-show day.

Later that day before the *Les Miz* matinee, I didn't even have an appetite for lunch. I'd been nervous not knowing how my audition went, so my stomach was a little upset. Finally, by intermission, I got word that I had landed the role of Thuy in *Miss Saigon.* I was on top of the world. At twenty years old, I had just landed a principal role in a major Broadway musical premiere in Toronto. That was when it hit me, and I realized that I was exactly where I was meant to be.

In the short time I had before rehearsals started, I moved into a new apartment in Toronto's Cabbagetown neighbourhood. I also took some time to visit my parents, since they'd offered me some old dishes and cookware they had stored away in case anyone needed them. There was a noticeable change in their demeanour, like a sense of pride I'd never seen before. They seemed to show a real interest in how I was doing, and what was happening with the show, which was extremely gratifying.

Even when I was moving, they decided that they wanted to give me a hand, so they drove to Toronto to help me set up my place. My mum even sprung for a new bed, after having seen the state of the futon I'd been sleeping on for years.

I'd never had the chance to talk to them about our complicated past and how the many conflicts we had still affected me. As a result, it felt to me as though my parents had unilaterally decided that the past never needed to be discussed. In all honesty, I wanted nothing more than to believe that those things were far behind us, so I tried to ignore my feelings and just enjoy the fact that they seemed genuinely happy for me.

Miss Saigon started it's run with three full weeks of previews, which was unheard of in the early 90s. They had to make sure that there were no technical issues with the show and though things ran pretty smoothly, there were always risks associated with those types of productions. It had always been my opinion that the biggest problem with the mega musicals was that they had become almost too technical. Barricades, chandeliers, and turntable stages made it so that even the smallest of technical issues could cause the show to come to a grinding halt. For us, the helicopter was the biggest challenge, and there were more than a few times we stopped mid-show because of issues with it. By the time we got to previews, though, all the bugs had been worked out, and we were able to have a smooth opening night.

"Oh my God, Mum, what the hell is this?" I was trying to pry a long wooden object from where it had been wedged down the side of the box. "Is this what's making the box so heavy?" I asked as I finally pulled it free.

It was a large bamboo umbrella, much like a Japanese wagasa, and although I sort of knew what it was, I had no idea how or why it was there.

"Where did you get this, and why is it in here?

"Oh, that was the centre piece off the table."

"Centre piece? Like from a wedding?"

"No," she replied, "from our table at the *Miss Saigon* party."

"What?" I laughed. "Are you kidding me with this? You stole this from the *Miss Saigon* opening night party?"

"Other people were taking them."

"Yes Mum, but why do you still have it? And if you liked it so much, why did you just shove it in this box?"

My mum looked at me and said very sweetly, "So you could have something to remember the show." I was speechless. She simply wanted me to have a keepsake, a lovely gesture that in that moment, absolutely meant the world to me.

The decision to invite my entire family to the opening-night gala was made in an attempt to not exclude anyone. It was my way of trying to set aside the past and move forward. Part of me wanted my family to see my success as proof that they had been wrong about me, and that in spite of all that I'd been through, I'd managed to become successful.

The truth of the matter was, I'd have been happy to only have my sister there, since she had been the most important part of my life, as well as the most supportive. Even through high school when she was busy trying to carve out her own path, she would always make time for me. She would often sit and talk to me about how I was doing, or ask how she could help. I know she didn't like what had happened to me, but I also know how powerless she felt to do anything about it. Now a busy officer with the Hamilton Wentworth Regional Police department, and thriving on her own, she was still always there for me, and I couldn't think of a better way to show my pride and appreciation than to share that moment of my life with her.

I hired a limousine to pick my whole family up from Hamilton and bring them to the show. It made things much easier for them, as well as more exciting. My mum had never been in a limo before and was thrilled at the idea of taking one for a night on the town.

It was an extraordinary once-in-a-lifetime event that saw me treated like some kind of celebrity for the evening. I was constantly being whisked off by the press for photos or being interrupted mid-conversation to be introduced to various people from New York and London. All the attention made me feel slightly uncomfortable, but I accepted it as part of the business.

There was an executive producer from New York who'd approached me and was extremely complimentary of my performance. I thanked him, and as he walked away, my older sister's husband, my ignorant hick of a brother-in-law, asked me if he was a "fairy." I had been caught off guard at first, but not overly surprised as the multitude of homophobic comments he'd made to me over the years came flooding back. Beyond enraged, I should have called him out on his bullshit right then and there, but not wanting to create a scene, I chose not to respond. I'm not even sure what I would have said since my mind was in a million places that night.

In an act of defiance against his disgusting slur, I accepted an offer to slow dance with an extremely handsome male dancer from the National Ballet of Canada. Confident that my whole family could see me on the dance floor, I didn't need to look for any reaction. With the exception of that incident, the evening was a huge success, and the following day, the reviews of the show as well as my performance were overwhelmingly positive.

It had all been a whirlwind leading up to the opening night, and once it was over, I had to find a way to settle into the run of the show for another year at least. Thanks to my bigot-in-law's rancid behaviour, though, I decided that it would be best to put a little distance between me and my family.

The cast of the show was very young, especially the leads who were mostly all under twenty-one. There was a lot of pressure on us to carry a show at that age, and before long, I noticed the cracks beginning to show. One of the other lead actors was struggling both vocally and emotionally, and because of my own experiences, I understood completely how they were feeling. Hoping to make a connection between the two of us, I had confided in them that I'd felt pressure and anxiety about my performances and that I often suffered from panic attacks. I thought it might help them to know that they weren't alone.

Things reached a critical point for the actor when, during an evening performance fairly early on in the run, I started to notice that something wasn't quite right. There seemed to be much more emotion than usual, as well as overly strained vocals that I would never have expected from someone with such a strong and soaring voice. Most everyone could see it was clear the actor couldn't possibly continue, and we wondered if they'd be pulled from the performance for the second act. There had been talk backstage about putting on an understudy, but management decided to keep things going as they were. In my opinion, they had done an otherwise wonderful actor a great disservice by forcing them to continue. By the time the last curtain fell, there was a collective feeling of relief among the entire cast, but my guess was that the effects of that trauma would haunt the actor for years to come.

It was an introduction to a dark and ugly side of the business I was unaware of. The demands of performing in these long-running productions could be extremely stressful, something most actors didn't talk about. As a result, I stayed pretty quiet about my own struggles, inevitably making things more difficult for myself. Even though I was pretty good at hiding it, the anxiety made it hard not to start thinking of the show as "that thing I had to do at the end of my day," most of which was spent preparing.

Every actor has their own process, and because of my panic attacks, mine consisted mostly of relaxation techniques. *Saigon* wasn't an overly physical show for me, but I spent a great deal of time preparing my body using yoga in combination with breathing exercises. My role in the show was vocally demanding however, and to warm up my voice, I'd start vocalizing in the early afternoon, and continued after the half-hour call when actors needed to be in the theatre before each performance.

Despite my daily efforts, the emotional toll the show was taking on me was getting progressively worse. Relying so much on my past trauma during my performances allowed my anxiety to grow out of control. There had been weeks where the panic attacks happened so frequently and so intensely that I could hardly summon the strength to go onstage. By that point I knew I couldn't keep going down that path, and I decided to seek out professional help.

There was a psychiatrist in a western suburb of Toronto that I saw on a weekly basis to try and get a handle on the situation. After a few months, there hadn't been any significant changes, and although I'd acquired a few temporary coping techniques, I was prescribed some medication for the times when I found myself in an overly stressful or panic-stricken situation.

I never discussed my anxiety and panic attacks with my parents, not that they would have been helpful in anyway, since my psychiatrist had suggested that a lot of what I had been experiencing was a result of unresolved issues from my childhood. Not wanting to jeopardize the fragile, albeit superficial relationship that we'd been building, I decided to keep it hidden from them.

I was painfully aware that it would take some time with the psychiatrist, but I was determined to put an end to the constant upset. Even if I had to confront some very uncomfortable aspects of my past, I was prepared to do whatever it took to rid myself of the overwhelming fear and anxiety.

At the end of my first year in *Miss Saigon*, I was offered a role in the revival of *Show Boat,* but my casual mention of it to our stage management team resulted in a rather expedient phone call from our creative team in New York. I was asked to reconsider the offer, and if possible, hold off on leaving *Miss Saigon*. Apparently, the producers had a surprise for me, and although it couldn't be discussed at that moment, I was meant to trust them.

After weighing all my options, I asked my agent to politely decline the offer for *Show Boat*, to which they graciously indicated I'd be kept in mind for later replacements or touring. It was a relief, knowing I wouldn't have to attempt to cross any burnt bridges in the future, especially with such large production companies.

Months later, I received a call from one of *Miss Saigon*'s associate producers in New York to discuss the surprise they had mentioned. The producers had decided to do a new symphonic recording of the show in its entirety, with a seventy-three-piece orchestra and an international cast. For this recording, I was asked to play Thuy, the role I'd been playing for the last year in Toronto. It seemed almost unreal to me at the time that I'd be playing a lead on a cast album of a Broadway musical. I could hardly contain my excitement.

Shortly after, I was flown out to New York to record my tracks. I had never been in a professional recording studio before, and didn't know what to expect. The idea of cast members recording separately was somewhat strange because I'd always assumed everyone would be all together. I was only the second person in the studio, which meant I was left to record my parts without most of the characters that I interacted with. In the beginning, I was having a bit of difficulty, but the musical supervisor came out of the booth and held my hand during some of the more dramatic scenes to help me achieve the intensity we were looking for.

At the end of the day, he was impressed with my performance, and I left the studio feeling stronger and more self-confident than I had in years, and even more so when the CD was released in 1995 to some critical acclaim.

I was finally coming into my own, and when I'd considered where I had been just a few years earlier, homeless and struggling, I would never have anticipated being where I was in that moment. Secretly, I'd always felt a sense of vindication when letting my parents know about new developments in my career, and the recording had been a real highlight. It was a sort of private "fuck you" in light of how I'd felt over the years, and I savoured every minute of it. Once and a while, when I was able to go back to

Hamilton, it was just to visit, and definitely not to rub their noses in it.

While in Hamilton, I'd also visit my best friend from high school who at that time was in the military, waiting for assignment. He'd been dating a girl he wanted me to meet, and on the occasions when I did, she seemed quite lovely. Eventually, when my friend had been deployed to Croatia on a peace keeping mission, his relationship with her came to an end. Even though they'd called it quits, I kept in touch with her periodically since we'd gotten along so well.

On a late summer evening while in Hamilton for the funeral of a former high school classmate, I decided to give her a call. I was reeling from the tragic death of my friend, and thought it would be nice to see a familiar face before heading back to Toronto. A meal at a late-night breakfast place ended in the two of us talking for hours. We shared a lot about ourselves and found we each had difficult pasts. She learned a little about the complicated relationship I had with my parents, and I learned that she had previously been married and divorced. We also discovered our many common goals for our futures, and even though I hadn't intended to, I ended up back at her place and spent the night.

We continued seeing each other, and eventually found ourselves in a full-blown relationship, which was strange for me since I'd never dated anyone who wasn't black before. Her parents were from the Philippines, and I knew very little about the culture, but I was falling in love, and eager to learn. I hadn't initially noticed the similarities in our appearance until several of her family members asked me if I was Filipino. That gave me something new to think about when it came to our future together.

With any of my serious relationships, I always took into consideration how my kids would identify, if I was to have any. I certainly didn't want them to experience the same unpleasant feelings of not fitting in as I did. Most often I dated black women, so there wasn't really an issue. The odds were that our kids would more than likely look black. I hadn't planned on meeting and falling in love with someone outside my race, so I was now in unfamiliar, yet not unviable territory. When she suggested that we get married, I was confident that because we *did* look so similar, our children would look Filipino, and hopefully, identify as such. I didn't necessarily need my kids to identify with *my* ethnicity, but it was important that they had an identity and a community with which they felt they belonged.

Things were going so well for me, but still feeling distant from my parents, I used our engagement as an opportunity to try to get closer to them. Of course, my mum was thrilled about the wedding, and I tried to involve her in the planning as much as possible.

With my parents, things seemed good, but then they had often appeared that way on the surface. It seemed difficult for me to have anything deep and meaningful with them. It was as if we were living out some sort of fantasy relationship based on good times that we'd never actually had. I will admit that it felt pretty nice to feel like I was in such a good place with them, but was any of it real?

In 1995 at the age of 23, I was able to help plan and pay for an extravagant wedding. The event went off without a hitch. In fact, people talked about that wedding reception for months afterwards. But even when it was over, I still felt a great deal of stress from all the attention. Quite ironically, as an actor, the idea of always being in the spotlight felt a tad bit unsettling, but the constant demand to keep myself there was even more disconcerting. The anxiety that I was still learning to deal with was very much front and centre and seemed to be progressively getting worse.

A month after the wedding, we discovered that my wife was pregnant, and I simply couldn't understand how it had happened. Not literally of course, (my mum had that talk with me when I was twelve). I just thought that we'd been so careful. She eventually admitted to me that before the wedding, she'd stopped taking birth control in an attempt to lose weight so that she'd fit better into her dress. I was shocked. Although I'd always wanted to be a father, I was terrified that not only was I not ready, but I was unsure what kind of father I would be. As a child I was afraid of my dad, and I had a genuine fear that with my own kids, I would react as he did and lose my temper in certain situations. After all, I'd had so much difficulty controlling my own emotions when I was younger that it was possible I'd have the same trouble as an adult.

It was a turning point in my life where I was given a unique opportunity to put an end to what I believed was a cycle of generational trauma. The question was, could I be the more empathetic communicative father that I'd always wanted? I found that I was confident enough in myself that I'd be able to rise to the occasion. And with that, my anxiety over the situation melted away, leaving me with only the feeling of excitement at the idea of being a dad.

Miss Saigon was coming to an end in Toronto, but fortunately, the producers wanted me to join the Los Angeles company, which was actually the U.S. First National touring production which had opened in Chicago in 1992. It was going to set up in LA for nine months and then would return to Chicago to start a new tour.

With the new gig, I'd be employed for at least another year or more, but I'd have to deal with the fact that I'd be away from home. Having toured before, I wasn't entirely sure I'd be able to handle a peripatetic lifestyle so early on in my marriage, but my wife and I agreed that taking the job would be good both professionally and financially, especially with a little one on the way.

Miss Saigon closed in Toronto on April 30th, 1995; Twenty years to the day of the historic fall of Saigon. There was no doubt I'd miss the Princess of Wales Theatre and the cast that I had grown so fond of during our time together, but I was heading off to Los Angeles to start a new adventure.

To say I was nervous about making my U.S. debut would be an understatement. I still had a little voice in my ear trying to convince me that I wasn't good enough, but I used only my good experiences with the show up to that point to prove to myself that I deserved to be there.

On my opening night in LA at the famous Ahmanson Theater, I felt my anxiety starting to get the better of me, so I spent a great deal of time quietly alone in my dressing room trying to focus. Although I had never been overly religious in the past, my struggles with anxiety had seen me become somewhat more spiritual. As a recovering Catholic, I still found comfort in the meditative properties of prayer, and before each show, praying the rosary helped to focus my attention and energy.

As I became more comfortable with the new cast and crew, my anxiety decreased significantly, and I started to feel a lot more like my old self. Rarely having to rely on my medication, I'd comfortably made it through the run in Los Angeles, and I was excited to move on to the next city and begin our year-long tour.

Next stop was Chicago, and during an evening performance in early November, my wife called into my dressing room from Toronto and had my dresser relay the message to me that our baby was on the way. I opted to skip the curtain call that night, and my saint of a dresser even drove me to the airport. We set off for O'Hare, manoeuvring at some pretty crazy speeds, and in an attempt to bypass the traffic, she may or may not have driven on the shoulder for a significant portion of the trip. We did manage to get to the airport in one piece and on time for me to catch the red-eye back to Toronto.

It was a very difficult labour and delivery. Our baby went into distress, which led to an emergency C-section. Completely distraught, I sat with tears streaming down my face as I was forced to wait in the hallway for what seemed an eternity. When I was finally allowed back into the room, they had just delivered our beautiful baby girl, and though I tried to see her, she was immediately rushed away by nurses. The room seemed disturbingly quiet while we waited for our daughter to be checked over, and holding onto my wife's hand in anticipation, I squeezed it tighter as every silent second passed.

Finally, after hearing a weak little cry come from the other side of the room, a wave of relief washed over me. I smiled at my wife and wiped away both our tears. I'd never loved her more than in that moment when our daughter let us know that she was okay.

My family came to visit us in the hospital, and to see their new granddaughter. Once again, I could see them display that newly familiar sense of pride.

When my sister held my daughter for the first time, she cried as she said to me, "It's another one of us." I'd never thought of it that way before, but my sister was right. For the longest time, it had just been her and me, but the idea of another little person sharing our DNA made me tear up as well.

After several weeks, when my daughter was able to travel, I brought her on the rest of the Saigon tour. Being so small made her extremely portable, and fairly easy to travel with. After healing from her C-section, which seemed to take longer than anticipated, my wife was able to actually enjoy the travelling as well, although as the workaholic she'd always been, it took a while for her to stop continually thinking about her job in the high-stakes world of finance waiting for her back home in Toronto.

I talked to my mum quite often while on tour, mostly to alleviate her worries about how we were handling being on the road with a newborn. I assured her that we were fine, and that our daughter had been amazing, even during all the flights.

I'm not sure who convinced who, but my parents decided to take a road trip and visit us in Chicago. It took them about nine hours to drive the whole way, but I was happy they'd come to visit. They stayed at a nearby hotel and spent some wonderful quality time with their new granddaughter. They got to tour the city and watch the show, which they loved seeing in the historic Auditorium Theater.

It was one of the first times that I'd felt my parents really being there for me, and wanting us to become closer. It's something I'd really wanted too, so I tried to involve them in our daughter's life as much as I could.

Being a dad was amazing, but touring with a newborn came with challenges. Navigating bottle sterilization, night-time feedings, and diaper changes all while doing eight shows a week took some getting used to, and it was quite tiring. At one point, I found myself so exhausted that when I'd stopped into the late-night grocery store just below our apartment, I had forgotten what I'd gone in for. After wandering the store for a few minutes, I remembered to get some eggs for breakfast, and formula for my daughter who was strapped to my chest in her harness, allowing me to shop more freely. I hadn't realized how out of it I must have looked until I got to the checkout and the woman behind me asked if I was okay. Jokingly, she remarked that I looked like shit, and when I turned around in shock to reply, she introduced herself as an actress who was appearing in the tour of *Grease* and staying in the same apartment complex.

She'd recognized me from *Miss Saigon* and thought to comment on how cute my daughter was and how she figured I probably wasn't getting much sleep. I sighed in agreement, as I waited for her to finish checking out. Then we both entered our building and got on the elevator. As she got ready to get off on her floor, she told me that she thought I must have been doing a great job with my daughter, because being on the road was tough as shit, regardless of how glamourous some people thought it was.

Later on, I realized that I'd picked up the wrong baby formula at the store, and that the one I was now feeding my daughter was one that had been fortified with iron. I guess I was too tired to notice at the checkout, which was a mistake I paid for during my daughter's three constipation-filled days that followed. She was right, I thought to myself. Being on the road is tough as shit.

We had very few difficulties through to the end of the tour in Vancouver, B.C., where I enjoyed the last few months of my time with the show. In the tradition of the Broadway Show League, I spent a large part of that summer playing baseball in tournaments against other shows touring through Vancouver, like *Showboat* and *Sunset Boulevard*. It was a wonderful way to spend time with the cast and crew, before we said goodbye.

During those final weeks, I had a final callback for the premiere of the musical *Ragtime*. I'd auditioned for the show earlier that year, but now had to fly to Toronto from Vancouver to be seen by the full creative team of the show. It was odd having to make the trip with my daughter, and when I showed up to the audition pushing a stroller and carrying my music book in her diaper bag, I had to ask reception to watch her while I went in to sing.

I received a positive response from the creative team and the show's writers, and although I didn't book the show, I was left feeling confident in my abilities since it wasn't common to hear much feedback at an audition, let alone something positive.

Back in Vancouver, I made sure to enjoy my final weeks of the tour. Both the show and my role in it had been a huge part of my life for four years, and it was very difficult to say goodbye.

Closing night was held at the Vancouver Aquarium, which amazingly, had been completely blocked off for our use. Talking with another cast member with a drink in my hand, I tried to look casual as I pointed out the killer whales that were swimming past us in an enormous tank next to where we stood. It was an incredible moment that I didn't take for granted, because it was quite possible that I'd never have an opportunity like that again. I was altogether so moved by the affection I was shown by the company, even though I hadn't been one of its original cast members. For years I'd struggled with feelings of inadequacy, especially with those closest to me, but in a profound moment of validation, the cast of the tour made me feel like a part of a very special family.

Thinking my time with *Miss Saigon* was over, I was ready to head home, to be with my actual family; my wife and daughter.

9

CLIMBING UPHILL

The First National Tour of *Miss Saigon* had been closed for about two weeks when I got a call from the casting director in New York about being in the show's Netherlands premiere. I was a bit tired, to be honest, but with the request coming from the top, I didn't want to piss anyone off, and so I signed up for another "tour of duty." The call came on a Friday, and they needed me to fly out to the Netherlands the following Monday, which left me limited time to pack, and worse, little time with my wife and daughter.

Of course I let my parents know that I would be heading overseas, and even though they agreed it was a good career opportunity, they wondered how it would be for my daughter. They felt it wasn't good for me to be away from home for too long, and they definitely weren't shy about telling me. It hadn't been the first time they'd given unsolicited parenting advice, having been overly critical of me taking a newborn on a U.S. national tour.

I reassured them that there was no cause for concern, and that I would have my daughter with me for a lot of my time in the Netherlands while my wife was back in Toronto working. Contractually, I had a sitter come to my dressing room to watch her while I was onstage. A friend had done it with her daughter on a tour, and it was something to which the Dutch production company had begrudgingly agreed to with me.

In fact, the company seemed to resent a great many things about having to hire me in the first place, the worst of which was my salary. The Netherlands had no union for actors, so they weren't bound to specific salary minimums. Coming from the U.S., I expected a salary to at least match what I'd previously made on the show, which the Dutch production company felt was ridiculous. Having no other choice but to agree to my compensation, they tried to make things difficult for me at every turn, often not following through with things that had been contractually agreed upon.

This treatment wasn't exclusive to me. The cast that was hired from the Philippines had their own issues about how they were treated. Cognizant of the fact that only cast members of colour were the ones having any difficulty with the production company, a startling pattern started to emerge. For the Filipino cast members, the pay inequity, and the living arrangements, made it all too clear the disparity between the Dutch cast members and the cast members who were persons of colour. Dealing with that shit back home was bad enough, but I had no idea that it could be worse elsewhere.

When I first arrived at rehearsals, I was handed the script and score which seemed weirdly unfamiliar to me. It was written in Dutch, something that posed a slight problem since I didn't speak the language. Although it didn't seem too much of a concern to the production company, I was completely stressed out as I had to attend Dutch language classes every day during rehearsals.

I couldn't remember a time I'd been that nervous, and I was almost certain that my anxiety attacks would be extremely difficult to control if I didn't start to feel more comfortable with the text. I spent a lot of time learning the show phonetically with the help of other cast members, and by opening night I managed to pull off what I honestly thought would be impossible.

While my parents missed their granddaughter, they continued to be very vocal about my parenting. My mum in particular often spoke about how my daughter needed more stability and structure in her life, and that my lifestyle wasn't conducive to raising a child. More than slightly offended, I explained to her that my daughter was doing quite well, and that there was no reason to worry. I may not have had the work schedule that most people had, but it was simply different, and it worked just fine for us. As a result of the constant commentary on my child rearing, I decided once again to put a little more distance between us, although I figured that the four thousand miles we already had should have been enough.

My wife would come and visit when she could, but I don't think she enjoyed the Netherlands very much. We tried to make the best of the awkward situation there by finding things to keep us busy. And busy we were. So much so in fact that it was no big surprise when my wife became pregnant again. We often joked that we had a kid "made in Holland," and it was a welcome surprise at a time when my stress levels were pretty high.

The timing of the pregnancy couldn't have been more perfect though, as the baby was due at the end of my contract, which in addition to how I'd been treated, made me all the more excited to leave the Netherlands.

A few months into the run of the show, one of the leading actors left. Surprisingly, he was replaced with another American who had done the show in New York. The two of us knew of each other, but had never actually met until then. We had a lot in common, since we were both from the U.S. and we both had daughters. He was half black and half Filipino, and oddly enough, we even shared the same birthday. He made the show much more bearable for the remainder of my time there, and I was honoured to have had the chance to call him my friend.

As wonderful as he was, he was also a very complicated individual. We spent a great deal of time together, often hanging out in Amsterdam where he was living. We'd head to museums and restaurants, and had a really good time exploring the city. Eventually, he confessed that he'd developed feelings for me, to which I really didn't know how to react. It must have been very difficult for him to open up like that, and I didn't know what to say. He was a very attractive man, and we got along very well. Had I not been happily married, perhaps I might have pursued him, but the truth was, I just didn't feel the same way about him. Weirdly, I recall asking him what he saw in me. A strange thing to ask, but in retrospect, I could see that I was still dealing with self-esteem issues. Ultimately, I ended up handling the situation poorly, constantly finding reasons not to hang out with him anymore.

To be honest, I was a pretty shitty friend, and instead of dealing with the matter maturely, I decided to simply avoid him whenever possible. Of course, it was easier when my wife would visit, because I'd be preoccupied with family, which was a valid distraction.

The best way I found to keep my mind off things was focusing on my physical fitness and dance training. I became extremely religious about going to the gym, and back to the dance studio which I had neglected for far too long. I was extremely fit, and was developing much more stamina in dance class. But I discovered, quite unfortunately, that my physical appearance was more important than I had initially anticipated when it came to my career. Before the show's Toronto closing a few years earlier, for instance, I was told quite publicly at a reception that I needed to lose weight before heading to Los Angeles. At the event, an associate producer from New York yelled at me from across the room: "Hey, you better lose some fucking weight before you get to LA." I was mortified and immediately recalled the humiliation of being teased by my asshole brother-in-law growing up. Quite ironically, I was being shamed by the very same associate producer whose sexuality was disgustingly derided by my idiot-in-law at the opening night gala in Toronto. It was particularly hurtful being attacked by someone whom I'd defended just a few years earlier, but even worse was that those few hurtful words were what started my unhealthy obsession with exercise and an eventual eating disorder.

I had lost quite a bit of weight while on the U.S. First National Tour, but in the Netherlands, I'd lost an unhealthy amount. No matter how much I worked out, I still saw a fat person in the mirror. Working out seven days a week, and at the dance studio for at least five, seemed a completely reasonable schedule, and while I admit that it felt nice being told that I looked good, I felt tired and extremely unhealthy. I wasn't eating enough for sure, and when I was having a particularly fat day, or I'd eaten something I shouldn't have, I would often resort to vomiting as a way of literally balancing the scales. I never realized the problem with what I was doing, because to me, the name of the game was losing weight, and keeping it off at any cost.

Whenever I'd be home, I usually received positive comments from people, but on one particular visit, my sister mentioned that I was looking a little too thin. I should have listened to her then, but I didn't think she was really being serious. She'd had her own struggles with weight when she was modelling, and it was possible that she was concerned I might be falling into some similar behaviours, but I rejected that idea. There was no way I was too thin. After all, I saw the fat when looking at my reflection. I paid no attention to what she'd said, and assumed she was only joking around. So I continued with my workout regime and strict diet, unaware that what I'd thought was the best thing for me was actually making me sick.

Originally, I agreed to stay in the Netherlands until my wife's due date, but as that day drew closer, and I still had no replacement, I agreed to return to the show for a maximum of two months after our baby was born. It would give them ample time to coach my understudy and bump him up to play the role.

Finally, in August of that year, near the end of my contract, we welcomed our second beautiful daughter. I had flown home a day before the scheduled C-section, during which everything went as planned, and I stayed for a week to be with my family before heading back to the Netherlands to tie up loose ends.

While in Toronto, I'd heard that the show *RENT* was going to be making its Canadian premiere. It was the only new show being mounted in Toronto, and it had been the hottest ticket in New York at the time. I was anxious to have work when I got home, so I inquired with my agent about the casting. I was told that there would be a huge open call, and that they were looking for unknowns with a real bohemian feel to their look and sound. It would also be difficult to secure an audition time, as those slots were very few.

My agency submitted me, but I was rejected by the casting director who knew me from *Miss Saigon* in Toronto. She indicated that she wasn't interested because as she explained to my agent, she felt my voice was too "legit" and it wouldn't suit the show. What was it that attracted me to a career where you were often told you weren't wanted? It seemed to be a running theme in my life that I hadn't really noticed up until then.

My whole life I'd dealt with rejection. Not just from the numerous television and film auditions where I hadn't booked the job, but also from being abandoned, and adopted, bullied, and eventually left homeless. I'd always been left feeling that I had something to prove, and this situation was no different. It's one thing to present who you are and be rejected; it's another thing to be dismissed without the ability to prove what you're capable of.

My agency was adamant that the casting director wouldn't see me, but that I shouldn't worry, another show would maybe come up down the line. Against their wishes, I decided to take matters into my own hands. It was clear I was coming home from the

Netherlands, that much was sure, but I was determined to return with a gig.

As it turned out, *RENT* was also being mounted in the West End of London, and its casting was being done around the same time as Toronto. When I heard about the open call for the show's London premiere, I decided I'd take a chance. I booked a flight, and took a quick trip to the UK. It was a long shot, but it was definitely better than sitting back and doing nothing.

My assumption was that they'd be searching for unknowns as I'd been told they'd been doing in Toronto, so I created for myself a character who had no experience. I didn't know much about the show other than it was set in the East Village, New York, so I tried to dress in an appropriate bohemian style like I'd seen in some of the pictures from the show.

I showed up to the audition with no headshots, no resumé, and no music. I took a ticket, and waited outside in line for several hours. The mix of heavy rain and light drizzle almost made me give up twice, but eventually, I got to the front of the line.

The creative team asked why I'd decided to audition, and acting as though I'd never sung before, I replied that I thought it would be fun to try out for their play. After learning I had no music with me, they were kind enough to ask if I knew the song "Amazing Grace." I told them that I was willing to try, and I shyly walked over to the accompanist. After being handed the lyrics to the song, I politely asked him to follow along with me, while in my best pop and R & B style, I belted out *"Amazing Grace"* with all the soul of a sinner testifying in church. And when I'd finished, the panel asked me to learn some music from the show and come back and see them the next day.

I'd got through the first round, so I was super excited, but I was left having to find somewhere to stay in London since I hadn't anticipated a callback. Booking what I can only assume was a reasonably priced hotel in London, I headed out for food and to see if I could find the soundtrack for the show. With sheet music and CD in hand, I headed back to the hotel to settle in for the night.

The following day, I arrived at my callback only to discover that the U.S. casting team was in the room, and when I finished singing from the show, I was asked once again to come back and learn music for one of the lead roles. Because I needed to get back to the Netherlands, I had to come clean and explain everything. The act I'd been putting on pretending to be a random inexperienced bohemian had to come to an end. I informed them that I was from Toronto, and how I'd gone to London because I wasn't able to get an audition back home. The New York casting team asked if I would be interested in doing the show in Toronto, to which of course I said yes. They took down my agency's contact information and told me they'd see me there.

Before long, I was on a plane back to Toronto to sing for the director and musical director. As frazzled as I'd been from all the travelling, I must have made a fairly decent impression, because the following week, my agency called to let me know that I was going to be in the show's Canadian premiere at Toronto's Royal Alexandra Theatre. It was a relief to be going home to a gig, and understanding that it was one that was coveted by many other actors, I was extremely grateful for the opportunity to be a part of *RENT*.

There was just enough time before rehearsals for my wife and I to move into the new house we'd purchased in an eastern suburb of Toronto. Living in my downtown three-story walk-up had become a nightmare with such small children, and we definitely needed more space.

The suburbs weren't really my thing, but living close to my wife's parents was incredibly helpful since they could give us a hand during the week when my wife and I were at work. Logistically, it was an ideal situation that we decided to take advantage of.

I know that my mum and dad felt slighted at the idea that we were moving even further from them, but given some of my mother's criticism of my parenting, and the stress of starting a new show, I was more than happy to entertain fewer visits.

10

WHAT I DID FOR LOVE

"You never liked this show, did you?" I flipped through the playbill for the Toronto production of *RENT*. I knew what my mum's answer would be, but I wanted to hear her say it.

"It was okay," she said. "Not quite what I'd expected, I guess. I'm sure I would have liked it if I'd seen you in it."

"No, I don't think you would've," I replied, and smiled to myself at the compliment.

It was nice of her to say, although I knew it wasn't the truth. I'd told my parents that the show had been dubbed the *Hair* of the '90s, and since they'd seen that show twice in 1969, coincidently also at the Royal Alex, I thought that they might at least appreciate its social significance.

Actually, I felt the show's message of living each day to the fullest, in response to poverty, homelessness, and living with HIV was moving, and although I was terribly nervous about my job in the show, I was nonetheless excited. I was hired as a swing and an understudy for the role of Angel, a street performer and drag queen. Understudying wasn't new to me having already done it in *Les Miz*, but being a swing was something I'd never done. Because I knew it would be a stressful and often thankless job, I wasn't sure I'd be able to handle it. Swings are cast members who are tasked with learning several roles in a show, and although they are required to be at the theatre for each performance, there are no guarantees that they'll be on. Because of the nature of their job, they have to be ready to go on at the drop of a hat should someone become unable to perform for one reason or another.

By the time we opened, I knew the show inside and out since I'd been on for all six of the characters I covered while the show was still in previews. In fact, I was on more often than not which anyone who'd ever been in the show would know was pretty much the status quo for RENT. I ended up being able to hold my own during the run, and actually survive to tell the tale.

I hadn't invited my parents to see the show because they'd had tickets through a tour group for seniors that they belonged to. The group would get together every month and have some sort of outing that often included watching a show in Toronto.

Unfortunately, as luck would have it, when the group eventually came to a matinee performance, I wasn't on that day. I met my parents and their group at the intermission, and I could tell my mum was less than impressed. I'm not sure if it was the subject matter, but the whole group didn't seem to enjoy it very much.

I felt a little embarrassed as I watched my mum trying desperately to convince her friends that I was an integral part of the show, even though I wasn't on that particular afternoon. As she explained to them that I was usually on, and that my job in the show was very important, I wasn't entirely sure who she was trying to convince. I know that she was disappointed that she didn't get to see me perform, but it was painful to watch her struggle to find a way of impressing her friends.

The show continued to run in Toronto, and I would commute by train forty-five minutes to and from the suburbs every night. It was a good schedule, especially since it let me stay at home with my daughters during the day while my wife was at work.

Since our only matinee days were on the weekends, I felt almost like a stay-at-home dad who just happened to work in the evenings during the week. And, because I'd made friends with some neighbours on our street, I was able to set up play dates with the other parents, giving me a good chance to socialize, which I enjoyed.

After almost a year of my suburban routine, the show announced its Toronto closing, and its subsequent small Canadian tour that would end in Vancouver. The tour was short enough that I would be back home for the Christmas holidays, which was perfect.

Returning directly home after the tour was a real privilege because my career hadn't afforded me much downtime in the past. That's why I cherished absolutely every minute I got to spend with my family. Seeing my wife felt almost bittersweet though, because for several months I could feel us starting to drift apart, and I struggled to understand what I may have done to push her away. She'd always made it clear to me that she was fine with the fact that I would have to travel for work, but when we would see each other after having been apart for long periods, she seemed distant, and even went to great lengths to avoid intimacy.

For a while, I felt as though she wasn't physically attracted to me anymore, which fuelled my body image issues even further. There was barely an ounce of fat on my body, but I pushed myself harder and harder, hoping that eventually, she would find me attractive again.

In my life, I'd often been made to feel that if something was wrong, I was most likely to blame, so I never considered that the problem could have been something else entirely. It was possible that my wife had been dealing with some things of her own. She'd often mentioned feeling self-conscious about weight she'd gained while pregnant with our youngest daughter, but I tried to reassure her that I always found her attractive and loved her at any size.

Because I was in no hurry to get back to work after the tour, I figured it would be the perfect opportunity to spend some quality time reconnecting with my wife over the holidays.

Christmas had always been my favourite time of year, and having kids of my own made it all the more special. Normally, we didn't have many opportunities to visit my mum and dad, but I was always happy to take the kids to visit them during the holidays. Even though my relationship with my parents was complicated, it didn't have to be that way for my girls.

That year, we'd had a lovely visit that was unfortunately, but not unexpectedly, cut short by my wife's desire to leave. She never liked visiting my parents, and I'd come to expect that at some point during a visit, she would feign some sort of illness. Allergic reaction to the cat became a pretty standard one, although there were others to be sure. For the most part, I was fine to roll with it, because I wanted to make sure she knew I supported her.

When the dust of the New Year's celebrations had settled, the reality of my unemployment sent my wife into a full-blown panic, and as a result, she asked her sister to find me a job at the mutual funds company where she worked. Some offence was taken, since it had only been a few weeks since I'd been home, but wanting to keep her happy, I swallowed my pride, and took a job in the mail room. I wasn't happy about it, but I did understand some of her valid concerns about my lack of employment albeit short lived.

This is when I began to see a very different side of my wife, a side that seemed to keep her totally preoccupied with money. Everything became about acquiring more stuff. She wanted the bigger house, the better car, things that I felt were unattainable both at our age, and our tax bracket. I had hoped that her fixation on material things would lessen after I found a new job, but somehow, I felt, it became even worse.

Almost immediately after taking the mail-room job, I auditioned for The Stratford Festival's production of *West Side*

Story. I made sure I was fully prepared, and was in pretty good shape, but when I was told to bring my knee pads to the audition, I took it to mean that either there were some questionable casting practices, or that the original Tony Award-winning choreography created by Broadway legend, Jerome Robbins, would be no cake walk.

I kept it together during the audition, and ended up being cast in the role of Chino. It meant that I'd have to leave my mail-room job only a few short weeks after I'd started, in order to make my Stratford Festival debut in their forty-seventh season.

I'd dreamed of performing at Stratford since the class trips I'd taken there as a child, and although I didn't really see people like me represented, I had always been fascinated by the spectacle. The Stratford Festival is the largest repertory theatre company in North America, and since it would be my first season, I hadn't been overly familiar with how it worked. During a season, actors are required to appear in at least two different productions, so while *West Side Story* was my primary show, I was also cast in several non-speaking roles in my secondary show, *The Tempest* which was being directed by the artistic director of the Festival. This opportunity was particularly exciting since Shakespeare was something I'd never done before. I was also tasked with doing a tertiary show, in which I was understudy for the title role in *Dracula: A Chamber Musical*.

There had always been a sense that actors in musicals weren't taken as seriously as those in the straight plays. This led to a constant need to prove ourselves, which was even more prevalent if you were an actor of colour, of which there were so few. It would be a challenge to prove that I was as good as any other members of the acting ensemble, but a challenge that I was willing to accept, especially if it meant opening doors that had once been closed to me.

The Festival itself was a very unique environment, and one that took some getting used to. The season would have barely begun when folks would start to speculate about what shows were being staged the following season. Of course, the biggest question on everyone's lips was, "Are you asked back?" You'd barely start one production when you'd start hustling for next year's gig. I was never sure what to make of it all since I didn't put much stock in those sorts of things. I'd always figured that if they needed me, I'd go back. I could see the stress it put on a lot of people and it felt like orientation at the Festival was a lot like a first day in prison. You needed to find out who to avoid, who could help you, and who did what for cigarettes.

There was also something odd about how so many of the same actors returned every season, and that there was a sort of hierarchy in the company which would determine who was coming back the following year. Depending on who you impressed, you could spend your entire career there.

On a hot summer night during an evening performance of *The Tempest*, our stage manager came rushing up to me as I was signing in at the call board. One of the Festival's biggest stars, and more importantly, a Canadian theatre icon, had requested to see me in his dressing room at intermission. All the blood drained from my face. I couldn't imagine why he'd need to see me; we weren't even in any scenes together. I kept running scenarios through my head to figure out what I may have done wrong, and what he could possibly have to say to me.

When the time came, I made my way to his dressing room and politely knocked. The door opened and a tall statuesque man with piercing eyes stood there looking down at me.

"Do come in," he said. I was nervous, and cautiously scanned the room as I entered. He had a nice lounge chair, I thought, and I remember him boiling the kettle for tea. They were pretty sweet digs as far as dressing rooms go.

"Is everything alright?" I asked.

"Yes, yes, it's fine. It's just that the director and I were discussing it, and in act two when you enter as a spirit to put on my robe…"

Like a bolt of lightning it hit me, and I knew exactly what he was talking about. The only business I had with him was when I would walk up behind him, put his robe over his shoulders, and exit stage right.

"When you put on my robe, we thought you should walk around in front of me and make sure that it is on securely. My character definitely wouldn't fiddle with it."

With that, he demonstrated by moving in close to me as he mimed adjusting the robe. I looked down at his hands which were now resting on my chest. I looked up into his eyes that continued to stare at me intensely. I'd heard rumours about this sort of thing, but I never thought it would happen to me. With his hands still on my chest, he said in a deep voice, "Shall we do it?" Oh my God! I thought. This is when he bends me over this chaise lounge, and if I let him do stuff to me, I get a better part next season.

With a small shaky voice I asked, "Do what?"

Expressionless, but continuing to look me in the eye, he said, "The robe!"

Whew, what a relief. He simply wanted to practice with the actual costume piece. I'd never felt more embarrassed. There I was, trying to avoid being violated, when the man just wanted to rehearse. I quickly practiced with the robe once, to which he said, "Thank you very much." And I was on my way.

Later, I wondered how I would have reacted if that interaction had actually turned inappropriate. Would I have said anything? Or worse, would I have let it happen? Thankfully, I wasn't literally put in a position where I'd have to make any of those decisions.

By the time my parents came to see *West Side Story*, I had just taken over the role of Bernardo. I replaced the original actor who'd left for New York to do another show. It was my first lead at the Stratford Festival, and I was happy to have my mum and dad there. My sister came to see the show as well, and it was nice to see that I'd impressed her. She told me she hadn't realized that I could actually dance that well, and though I'm not sure what she thought I'd been doing in my dance classes all those years, I took it as a compliment.

The Festival provided an opportunity to push myself creatively as an actor. I was given permission to make choices. And these choices weren't shot down because they weren't the same as how someone else had done it. We were encouraged to have creative input, with little to no unnecessary push back. The one caveat, though, was that although I tried bringing some dimension to my characters, I was still limited to playing the same somewhat stereotyped ethnic roles I'd been playing in the past. The amount of diversity in theatre was changing, but I began to think that the Stratford Festival was going to take a while to catch up.

At home, I was finding a nice work/life balance. My daughters weren't in school yet, so that summer they lived with me in Stratford. The small house I had rented was close to one of the theatres, and owned by a woman in town who had a diner that was frequented by many artists working at the Festival. We had a nanny that lived in the house, and helped out with the girls when I was performing a matinee, or at rehearsal. There were lots of things for them to do around town, and they even got to watch *West Side Story* a few times. Originally, I thought they'd be a bit young, but sitting so quietly during the performances, they displayed better behaviour than some of the students in the crowd of a matinee.

On several outings to the playground, my daughters would play their own little version of *West Side*. My oldest would play Maria, and my youngest was ordered to play Chino, to which she would always begrudgingly agree. I absolutely adored being with my girls, and moreover, generally enjoyed being a father. I felt very close to them, but unfortunately, I continued to feel that my wife and I were drifting further and further apart. I tried to spend time with her, both alone and with the girls, but she seemed to be all consumed with work. I never questioned anything that she wanted, yet I struggled to make her happy. And although I was irritated by some of her choices, I simply remained silent, knowing that as long as I kept working, and had a steady stream of income, she would be content. In hindsight, I realize that I felt that her love for me was becoming tied to my level of income and success. And of course, that brought me back to the terrible, yet not unfamiliar feeling of needing to constantly prove my worth.

When my youngest daughter had her second birthday that summer, my parents came to the large backyard party we had for her. I had hoped that seeing me in that environment with my friends and colleagues would show them how happy I was to have found a place where I truly belonged, and that I was thriving in all aspects of my life. It was nice to have them there, but I continued to feel that our relationship remained bereft of anything substantive. I'm not altogether sure what I expected of them, but as hard as I tried, I couldn't quell the feeling that I needed something more.

As my season at Stratford was winding down, I headed into my final callback for the Toronto production of *The Lion King*, the stage musical based on the 1994 Disney animated film. I had been in New York the previous year auditioning to replace the original Simba, and although they couldn't offer me the job then, the creative team expressed their excitement at seeing me again in Toronto.

There were so many people in the room when I arrived, but I hardly felt nervous at all. It was my fourth or fifth time seeing them, so I was getting quite used to being there. I thought I'd done extremely well, but when I finished, there was absolutely no feedback from the director. She just sat and scratched some notes on her bright-yellow pad, as her silence told me everything I needed to know.

After all the auditions, callbacks and feedback that indicated I was at the top of the list to play the part, I was asked to understudy the role of Simba, to which I politely declined. I had never turned down a job before, but because my pride had been wounded, I thought it was the best decision I could make in order to protect my feelings. That choice left me vulnerable since I'd never been without a gig to go to when another one was finishing. Not at least without an audition or two booked shortly thereafter. My season at Stratford was coming to an end, and because I'd developed a false sense of security over *The Lion King*, I was struggling with what I should do next.

While giving myself time to feel sorry for myself and mourn the loss of a great role, a friend of mine from London who was coming into Toronto asked to meet up for dinner and drinks. He was a musical director I'd known from *Miss Saigon*, and he was flying in to hold auditions for a show he'd arranged that was based on the music of ABBA. The show was called *Mamma Mia* and had opened in London to rave reviews.

When my agency reached out to inquire about the auditions, like a broken record, they were told by the same casting director of *RENT*, and *Miss Saigon*, that I wasn't what they were looking for. Luckily, with my friend as the show's musical supervisor, I was able to bypass Toronto casting, and I ended up being seen by the entire creative team. Despite originally being turned away, I was cast in the ensemble and an understudy for the role of Sky in *Mamma Mia*'s North American premiere. Once again, I'd found myself in another production at the Royal Alex, at least until we took the show to the U.S. to start its pre-Broadway tour.

Before rehearsals started, I got to enjoy doing typical dad stuff with my daughters, helping with homework and even volunteering at their school. I also tried to rekindle the relationship with my wife, which was made a little easier by the fact that she knew I had a contract about to start. Things improved between us for a little while, but it didn't seem to last. Something seemed off. The way she viewed me had changed, and I began to feel that work may have been causing her too much stress. My wife worked extremely hard and was amazing at what she did thus, people expected a lot of her. It was difficult for her to navigate pushing herself ahead in her career and spending time with us as a family.

Children see and hear everything, and are quite intuitive when it comes to matters of the heart, and my daughters were no exception. I hadn't realized it at the time, but they were able to articulate exactly what they thought of our family dynamic, even at a very young age.

In the family room one evening, I interrupted our usual game of "Power Rangers" to tell my girls that it was getting close to dinner time. Understanding what that meant, they started to tidy up, while my oldest daughter told me that we'd all need to help because "our" mom would be home soon.

"Our mom?" I asked. "What do you mean, *our* mom?"

Although they understood that I was their dad, it was also their understanding that their mom was also my mom, and at the top rung of the ladder. Effectively, the hierarchy was my wife, followed by me, then them. It was an interesting observation, and although it took a while, it eventually opened my eyes to what I believed was the biggest problem in our relationship.

11

SOMETHING WAS MISSING

Once again, the grandfather clock reminded us of the time. At this moment, only half the chime was played indicating that it was half past the hour, and more specifically, half past two. I heard the toilet flush upstairs, and I rolled my eyes at the idea that the bathroom was more an office for my father than his actual one.

"Why are you getting rid of this? I thought you were big fans?" I held up the ABBA *Gold* CD I'd come across, and wondered why they would get rid of a gift I was extremely proud to have given them. My mum moved her glasses a bit and squinted at the CD. "Oh, we already had that one, but we didn't want to just throw this one away."

"Are you crazy? You couldn't possibly have had this, it's the one that I gave you as a gift."

"I know, but I didn't have the heart to tell you, we'd already had it."

"It's not just the *regular* CD." I was starting to get a little annoyed. "It's the one I had autographed by Benny and Björn."

"Is that right," she said. "Give us it here then."

I handed her the CD as she proceeded to inspect it. I could see her scrutinizing the signatures, as if she was an expert in the field of document authentication.

"Oh bugger, I'd never noticed that before. We'll have to hang onto that."

I laughed a bit as my mum opened up the CD and continued to study it, as if it was something she'd never seen before.

One of the challenges of being in a new production was making sure it worked for its target audience. It was widely known that shows that started off and worked well in London, didn't always translate well on Broadway. *Mamma Mia* was the story of Donna, a middle-aged single mother. Her twenty-year-old daughter Sophie is getting married, and decides to invite three men from her mother's past, hoping that one will turn out to be her father. The show had done extremely well in London, but I had general concerns about the way it would be received in Toronto.

Surprisingly, the ABBA music seemed to flow seamlessly from scene to scene, which was refreshing, considering I had no idea how the book was going to work with the music. To be honest, I doubted that it would. I was under the impression that the audiences would somehow be too smart for the show. After all, it had somewhat of a cheesy quality to it that although I thought was fabulous, I wasn't really sure the audiences would feel the same way.

I held onto that feeling right up until our first preview, but by the end of the night, when the audience was on its feet, dancing and singing along, there was no denying that the show was a hit and I was in it.

The crowd went so crazy during the curtain call of the show, that as they were singing along and swaying back and forth, the upper balconies started to shake. As a result, the producers had to bring in a structural engineer to inspect the theatre for fear that they might collapse. The whole process took the better part of a day, but in the end, we were given the okay and we continued with the scheduled performances.

Again, when my parents came to the show, they were with their seniors' group, and I went to meet them at the stage door after the performance. My mum introduced me to a few of her newer friends that I hadn't met, and they all seemed to have loved the show. It was a much different reaction from when they'd seen *RENT*, and there was no shortage of congratulatory comments indicating to my parents that they must have been very proud.

Normally, those kinds of comments were lovely to hear, but it all seemed quite irritating then. When they'd come to see *RENT*, I wasn't performing, but this time, not only was I was on, but I was performing the role I was understudying. Now their friends, having actually seen me on stage, were gushing over my performance, and I could see how happy it made my parents.

I became triggered. I was clearly still holding onto the anger and pain of the past, and instead of just seeing my parents being happy for me, I saw what I thought was an air of false pride in having been responsible for who I was in *that* moment. I was where I was in that moment as a result of having overcome every obstacle thrown in my path, some by their own hands. Of course, it was their parenting skills that helped make me a stronger person, but in that moment, I just felt that they were taking too much credit for my success. Pretending as though nothing happened during my time with them growing up minimized the real trauma that I experienced as a kid, and its long-lasting effects.

Luckily, my parents were leaving with their group that day, because if I'd had to engage them privately after that, I might have said something I'd regret. Everything I'd thought to put into words that day would have to wait until I returned from the U.S. tour. At least with some time, I'd be able to calm myself and try to figure out why I felt this way.

Originally, *Mamma Mia* had been scheduled to run in Toronto for only six months, but in a bizarre turn of events, the skyrocketing ticket sales forced the producers to extend its run by having an entirely new cast take over for us when we headed out on the road. As our company was performing the show at night, a new cast was rehearsing on the set during the day in order to ensure a seamless transition. After a successful six-month run, we headed off to start the national tour leaving behind a new company of Mamma Mia, which would continue to play Toronto for another five years.

We were given a one-week vacation before heading to San Francisco, our first stop on the tour, and I was definitely going to need every day of it to pack up my life for a year on the road.

With the best of intentions, my wife thought that we should take that week for a family vacation. A wonderful idea, planned with the worst possible timing, although I could see that it was her attempt at trying to reconnect which I was definitely pleased about. Even though I tried to get her to reschedule the vacation, I found myself booked on an unexpected cruise to the Mexican Riviera. It was difficult for me to relax on that trip because I was so preoccupied with the upcoming tour, and making sure that everything was ok with the San Francisco sublet I'd found on Craigslist.

After the cruise, our flight had us arriving at the San Francisco International Airport on the first day of rehearsals at the Orpheum Theater. This gave me almost no time to acclimate to the city or to the new time zone. I was exhausted, and having been on a boat for a week, I was left with a significant degree of difficulty getting my land legs. Slightly annoyed, and completely disoriented, the flashing disco lights and choreography made it almost impossible for me to get through "Voulez-Vous," but as I powered through to the end of the number, I started to feel a little bit better.

On opening night, just as I was finally settling into the city and the new theatre, I received a message backstage explaining that my family wouldn't be seated because at three and five years old, my daughters were too young to watch the show. I was in absolutely no mood for such nonsense, and found it difficult to resist the urge to put up a fuss. Our company manager however, stepped in and got things sorted out, and just as I'd tried to explain to the front of house manager for eight solid minutes, my girls *were* able to sit through the show, quietly and respectfully.

The Opening in San Francisco was a huge success, but it came and went fairly quickly, which meant my wife and daughters would be heading home to Toronto, leaving me for a few months on my own.

When working on a show, it wasn't unusual for me to head straight home after each performance. I wasn't really one to hang out afterwards, especially after some of the questionable choices I'd made while doing *Les Miz,* but on tour without my family, I took the time to get to know the cast, and I'm so glad that I did. *Mamma Mia* was magical for many reasons, but mostly because of the friendships I'd developed over the more than two years I stayed with the show. Bonding with the company allowed me to see how people handled being away from their significant others, giving me insight to deal with my own relationship as my wife and I continued to have problems.

When the show was in Toronto, things were fine. I was staying home during the day with the kids, and I'd head into the city to do my show after my wife got home from work. Things felt strained, but we managed to keep it together for the most part. When I left for the tour, however, things got progressively worse. We barely had meaningful conversations, and although she was visiting fairly regularly, she always seemed to be unhappy.

That year on tour would have been my first time away from my family during the holidays, but because my dad's mother passed away just days before Christmas, I was compelled to head home for several days. After her lengthy illness, I liked to think that my grandma was doing me a solid by departing when she did, allowing me to spend the holidays with my family.

My parents seemed happy that I made it to the funeral, and I am glad I was able to let go of that feeling of anger I had backstage after they saw the show in Toronto. It was important that I be there to support my dad during that difficult time.

Years earlier when my other grandma passed, not going to the funeral had been a huge mistake. I should have been there to support my mum, but I let my pride get in the way, and made the situation all about me. My older more mature self knew better, and realizing how selfish I'd been back then, made me look at things quite differently now. In a way, this allowed me to come to terms with my absence from my other grandmother's funeral years earlier.

A week or two into our run in Los Angeles, I received a call from the Children's Aid Society in Ottawa. They had an update on a request my sister and I had placed months earlier for information about our biological parents. The request to track them down was born of a desire to confront some of our past trauma and hopefully get closure on some of the unanswered questions we had about why we were given up for adoption.

The CAS offered to conduct searches for the biological parents of any individual who had been adopted through their system, and regardless of the outcome, it was their policy to release to the adoptee any identifying information. Earlier I'd learned that prior to our placement in foster care, our mother had given up two other children for adoption. Potentially, my sister and I had four people to locate, but we were lucky that there were two of us looking. I'd chosen to search for our biological mother, and the sibling that was closest to my age, while my sister decided to have them search for the other sibling, as well as our biological father.

The CAS update showed that the search for our mother had turned up empty, but that they'd been in touch with a half-sibling who was born two years before me. Since this was the early days of mass access to email and the internet, we exchanged handwritten letters, and eventually spoke on the phone. It was an incredible experience finding a birth sibling, and quite shocking to learn that they had been living in Toronto for years. We could have crossed paths and never even known it.

In another unexpected turn of events, just a few short months after my grandmother had gone, my grandfather also died. I'd always assumed it was of a broken heart, as he and my grandmother had been married almost seventy years. I found myself back home for another funeral, but it also gave me the opportunity to meet my half-sibling for the first time.

We met at a downtown Toronto café where we talked for hours. I'd noticed that we shared very few physical similarities which didn't surprise me, because their birth father was white. I also discovered that not only had they been living in Toronto, but they had grown up just outside of Hamilton where I was raised. It was a lot to process in one meeting, and thankfully, we had many more meetings once I returned to Toronto from being on tour.

When my wife and daughters would visit me on the road, I tried to take them on as many outings as I could, but unfortunately, we'd always have to cut things short so that I'd have time to get to work. I tried to make my wife understand that although *she* was on vacation, I was not. I don't think it ever really registered with her that I was still working and had other obligations outside the performances each night. I couldn't just miss appearing on *The Tonight Show* with the rest of the cast because my wife wanted to stay at Disneyland a little longer. That's not to say I never took time off, but when I did, I preferred to spend time with my family, without the constraints of other responsibilities.

There were some things that were so important to me that I would schedule my vacation time around them. My favourite was always being there for my daughters' first day of school. In 2001, while the show was in Boston, I went home for a week to do just that. It was always bittersweet taking the girls to the school bus because although I was excited for them, I could also see how quickly they were growing up. My beautiful young girls, now ages four and six, were each developing their own identities, and I couldn't help but wonder who they would become.

As usual, my vacation week went by far too quickly, and as much as I hated to leave, I flew back to Boston on the morning of Tuesday, September 11th. Landing at Logan Airport just before eight o'clock in the morning, I got back to my apartment and started my regular routine. Making coffee and eating breakfast while watching a couple of episodes of the *The Golden Girls* on Lifetime. That was pretty much what I did every morning before going to the gym. As I flipped around the channels, I noticed some footage of the World Trade Center that I assumed was from the 1993 bombing. As I looked closer, I kept thinking how strange it was that the building was on fire so high up. I remembered that in '93, the bomb had gone off in the parking garage.

As I turned up the volume, I watched a plane hit the second tower. It took a moment, but it finally sunk in: this was happening live.

The first thing I thought of was the cast of the show. Most of them had gone to New York that weekend to see a dress rehearsal for the Broadway company, and I was worried that some of them might be caught up in the aftermath of everything going on. As the day progressed, it became increasingly difficult to reach anyone on their cell phones, and even though some of the cast tried for hours, nobody was getting through. Thank God I had my best friend in the show to be with all day. Having someone to cry with made things a lot less distressing.

Very late in the afternoon, I finally got in touch with my parents and let them know I was okay, and that they shouldn't worry. I don't know how long they'd been trying to reach me, but they knew I was flying that morning, and they were completely rattled when they learned that two of the planes involved had left from Boston Logan International. My dad's immediate reaction was to tell me to come home. He feared that as an American, I could be called up to serve, should the U.S. decide to go to war.

Numerous factors of uncertainty put my anxiety at an all-time high, and I'd become inundated with the news coverage which ran 24/7 on pretty much every television station. What was happening in the U.S. also introduced complicated issues to our show. Technically, we were a Canadian production touring the U.S., and many of the Canadian cast members were concerned for their safety should things escalate.

Things settled down after a few weeks, but trying to leave Boston to get to the next city on tour tested the limits of my self-restraint, especially when dealing with people's racial biases. As one of our cast members had so intuitively pointed out, my skin tone was going to make it difficult for me to pass through airport security. Painfully, they were right, and the number of times I'd been "randomly selected" for further inspection made me more than a little suspicious.

Having really no other choice, I accepted the fact that I would probably be subjected to the same thing everywhere I travelled for the rest of the tour. The situation was unfortunate, but allowed me to take stock of the things that I considered to be most important. My career was on the list, but not as high up as my relationship with my wife and daughters.

I was discovering that life was definitely too short to waste on work alone, and that there wasn't any real benefit in being away from my family. Knowing that I'd never get that time back, I decided to actively look for another job. One that would allow me to return home, and enjoy the life I'd been trying to build for the past several years.

My wife was not as keen on the idea of me leaving *Mamma Mia*, especially if any new job I found paid less than what I was making on the road. We often argued about it, which left me feeling as though we weren't really on the same page about our future anymore. There had been so much going on during that time, and fighting with her just added to my overall stress. Still, I had the gym to keep me focused, and poker night at my place with friends from the cast was always a welcome distraction.

Outside of my regular circle of friends on tour, I found myself getting close to another cast member during the aftermath of 9/11. Hanging out with her though, caught me more than a little off guard. During the run of the show in Toronto, she'd made several comments that led me to believe she wasn't overly fond of me, so I found it strange that all of a sudden, we were grabbing the odd dinner between shows, or hanging out sometimes on our day off.

I'm not sure at what point I figured it out, but I came to realize that she was attracted to me. I loved my wife, and had never considered getting involved with someone else, let alone someone I worked with. But I have to admit, the attention certainly felt welcome, especially since it made me feel desirable, which was something I hadn't felt in quite some time.

As a fellow performer, she appreciated my talent and related to me in a way that my wife couldn't. Her attraction to me was intense. In fact, I don't think my wife ever looked at me the way she did, and that attention was something that had been missing in my marriage, and I found it very difficult to resist.

Against my better judgement, I continued to spend time with her because I liked how she made me feel. My wife and I had been drifting even further apart as I continued to feel unseen and unappreciated by her, but as this new friend continued to be a supportive and understanding presence, I began to feel the shame of what I considered an emotional betrayal. The situation had become complicated, but by the time I realized I'd developed feelings for my co-worker, she'd decided to move on, and ended up involved with one of our stage managers. The entire situation was a mess, but it made me realize that while I enjoyed being the object of someone's affection, I wanted that someone to be my wife.

The need to be home for the sake of my marriage, and my sanity, became dire. So, disregarding my wife's appeals for me to continue on the tour, I finally made the difficult decision to look for another show. There was no way I'd be able to explain to her that I was leaving *Mamma Mia* without at least securing other work first. But as luck would have it, before officially giving my notice to resign, I'd been called back to Toronto to audition once again for the Stratford Festival.

The prospect of working there again was thrilling, and I went into the audition fairly confident, but a little nervous about doing a monologue from King Lear, which would be the featured play that season.

I knew I'd made an impression when just before leaving the audition, the artistic director pulled me aside to say, "you should do more of that." By the time we were in the next city of the tour, I received an offer from Stratford to appear in *Threepenny Opera*, and *My Fair Lady*, for their fiftieth anniversary season.

Giving my notice of resignation to *Mamma Mia* was difficult but necessary. I had been on a rollercoaster of emotion over those two-plus years with the show. I was finding family I didn't know existed, while slowly losing others. From the loss of my grandparents to the relationship with my wife, which was deteriorating to the point where I could no longer see our future together.

I desperately needed to be home where I could work through my feelings about my marriage, and being back at the Stratford Festival would give me the opportunity I needed while challenging myself creatively.

12

WE DO NOT BELONG TOGETHER

"A pyramiding combination of unfortunate circumstances…" is a line from *Threepenny Opera,* perfectly describing my experience in the fiftieth season at the Stratford Festival. Initially, it seemed like an amazing opportunity, affording me the ability to come home and be with my family. However, the season was riddled with problems for me right out of the gate.

Even accepting the Stratford contract was wrought with difficulty due to my wife's continued protestations. It was her concern that my salary was far less than what I'd made on my last tour, and because she'd become consumed by acquiring more and more financial wealth, it seemed my paycheque would never be enough, regardless of where I was working.

I took the job because it was the best decision for me emotionally, and if our marriage was going to survive, getting her onboard would be crucial. It took some time, but I managed to reason with her, and as genuinely concerned about our finances as she was, I thought she finally understood my need to be home.

As for the actual season, it was a challenge dealing not just with the shows, but some of the problematic members of the company. Perhaps it was because I was now officially in my thirties that I had become more sensitive to the behaviour of others, especially if that behaviour involved a certain level of ignorance.

The artistic director of the Festival was directing *My Fair Lady*, which was meant to be the highlight of the season. I learned a lot during the rehearsal process, most of which was constructive, but there were definitely some things of a more objectionable nature that I wish I'd never seen. Both myself and one of my closest friends in the show, who was also an actor of colour, bore witness to several disturbing situations that shouldn't have been acceptable at any time, let alone the fiftieth anniversary season. In a way, it felt like I'd been awakened from a deep sleep, only to find myself in 1952.

During a notes session after a full run of the show, our director launched into an anecdote about playing comedy. I'm not entirely sure what the point of the story was, but he obviously thought there would be value in telling it. Apparently, during a production at the Festival decades earlier, there was a scene with three young chorus girls who wore white powdered wigs with green grapes in their hair. "For some reason or another, it was hysterically funny," he chortled. "During the run of the show, one of the girls who was pregnant had to leave the show, and she was replaced by a "coloured." So, they decided to put red grapes in that actress's hair, and suddenly the audience didn't find it funny anymore."

I sat there completely perplexed. Immediately after the director used the term coloured, the entire cast turned to me and my friend, expecting to see some sort of a reaction of ire and outrage. What were we supposed to say? This was *the* artistic director of the Stratford Festival. No matter how we responded, it wouldn't have ended well. He was of a different generation, and even if we'd tried to explain why what he'd said was not okay, he'd more than likely have launched into a tirade of righteous indignation. Having to change because society had become overly sensitive was a tiresomely dramatic monologue I'd heard ad nauseam.

Every such offensive interaction seemed to involve males of a certain demographic, most of whom were the more "seasoned" of the Festival. One actor, for instance, requested that I meet him in his dressing room so he could show me something to which, "if seen without any explanation, I might take umbrage." Oh boy, I thought to myself, nothing good ever happened after an opening line like that. I couldn't wait to see what fresh hell was lurking just beyond his dressing-room door. Once inside, he proceeded to tell me that he had some special good-luck charms that he liked to keep on his dressing table. I was to understand, mind you, that even though he realized they were wholly inappropriate, they were nostalgic totems of his childhood in England. He then proceeded to point to a display case perched on his dressing table which contained an inordinate number of "golliwogs," which were dolls based on a black-face minstrel-type character from a nineteenth-century British children's book.

Before he could begin what I'm sure was a well-rehearsed history lesson in classic children's toys of Great Britain, I stopped him dead in his tracks and told him to "stop." Thanks to my Scottish mother, these were something I was already all too familiar with. My mum also had these ridiculously offensive items proudly displayed in our home. It was something that the two of us argued about constantly, as she too saw these repulsive caricatures as harmless childhood toys. I understood that it was only because she lacked the understanding of what they symbolized, that she exposed my sister and me to them unapologetically.

I stared at the vile little hate dolls, then directly back at him, then rolling my eyes I walked away, choosing not to engage. I'm not sure what he expected my reaction to be. I was definitely not the one to educate this idiot on the complicated history of his racist relics of yesteryear. I left it there, and simply avoided him for the rest of the season. I didn't have any scenes with him anyway, and I wasn't overly eager to start up another uncomfortable situation at this particular show. The cast had already dealt with some discourteous yet unsurprising behaviour from one of the lead actors to an understudy, so I felt no need to add this incident to the awkwardness already festering backstage.

Life wasn't much better over at the Avon Theatre, where twice a week, I was performing in *Threepenny Opera*. Our director, a seasoned actor himself whom I admired greatly, started off the first day of rehearsal by telling the cast members that he didn't like musicals. Unsurprisingly, things just went slowly downhill from there.

As a distraction from all the shit going down that season, I decided to take on the job of directing a fundraiser for The Performing Arts Lodge, the charity which built housing for retired and semi-retired entertainment industry workers. The cast and I had decided to do a concert version of *A Little Night Music,* an interesting choice as most everyone knew that the artistic director of the Festival was not a fan of Stephen Sondheim. The Festival gave me access to pretty much everything I needed, and the final product was a sold-out one-night concert event that was extremely well received.

It was such an amazing achievement for me that was sadly eclipsed by the never-ending relationship struggles I was having at home. Even on the night of the concert, my wife requested that we leave immediately after the show because she felt bored and tired. I resented not being able to celebrate the show's success with the cast afterwards. I just went backstage to congratulate and thank them, then headed straight home in disappointment.

I was extremely unhappy in my relationship, but instead of dealing with the situation head on, I blamed myself. As a result, I turned to alcohol in order to numb the pain while at the same time, avoiding confrontation at all costs. There was no way to know how long I could stay on such a self-destructive path, but full of self-loathing, I think I hoped to simply drink myself into a state of amnestic bliss. My focus became about my daughters, and making sure that they both felt loved and supported, something I wasn't entirely sure would happen if my marriage was to come to an end.

In the final months of the season, I had been deemed worthy of being "asked back," but this presented me with some logistical challenges that wouldn't be easy to deal with. Not only was I walking into a lead role in *Pericles*, something which was both exciting and scary, but I would also be playing a lead, as well as sharing the stage with both my daughters in *The King and I*.

Originally, I didn't want the girls, who were five and seven at the time to audition for the show, but since they'd asked, and showed so much enthusiasm, I decided it would be fine. Being cast wasn't a surprise to me because I was aware of their talent, but I was left having to facilitate their schooling, the show, and my wife simultaneously.

There was time over the holidays to work out the details, but in the meantime, I'd planned on having an amazing Christmas in the new house we'd bought two years earlier. I hadn't actually lived in it since coming off the road with *Mamma Mia,* and even though I went there on my days off, it wasn't quite the same. I was exhausted from the train wreck of a fiftieth season, and it seemed like the perfect time to relax a bit after not having had a real break in years.

My R and R was cut short when I was asked to understudy the role of Che in *Evita* in Winnipeg and Calgary during the holiday season. The offer was flattering, as I'd be understudying an amazing actor and friend, but to be honest, I wasn't really interested in taking on anything else before the start of my next season at Stratford.

Knowing how extremely busy I'd be balancing my daughters by myself, and the work I needed to do for the season, I simply wanted time to prepare myself for all that was about to land on my plate. My wife's suggestion that I do *Evita* was based purely on financial reasons, and to avoid any kind of confrontation, once again, I agreed.

Having very limited time to pack and get ready, I became both angry and resentful. I understood that taking that contract would quite possibly be the beginning of the end of my marriage, and with that, I began to fall into a deep depression.

I'd always considered my home and native land to be beautiful, but Winnipeg in the middle of winter was no picnic. The cold and dark of the city mirrored my overall mood, and it seemed that no amount of Canadian goose down could provide me the warmth I needed to summon the will to get out of bed every morning.

There was very little to do, and even spending time with the cast always led to us hitting the hotel bar a little too often. Almost every night was a night of binge drinking which was not a good look for a father heading into lead roles at the Stratford Festival with two daughters in tow. I slowed down my drinking a bit when the show moved to Calgary, and even though I knew I was developing a problem, I thought I would be able to just snap myself out of it. I was wrong.

As it happened, my wife was sent to Calgary on business, and she came to visit around the time of our anniversary. I made reservations at an Italian restaurant knowing Italian food was her favourite. Since we hadn't seen each other for almost a month, it seemed the perfect time for us to be alone and reconnect.

When we got back to my apartment, we were both so tired that we ended up going to bed fairly early, neither one of us expecting an overly passionate evening. When I moved my arm to embrace her as we slept, however, it sparked an all-too-familiar reaction.

"Just because I let you put your arm around me, doesn't make it an invitation...I'm not doing anything."

The humiliation was nothing I hadn't felt before, because for the last few years, she'd done her best to avoid intimacy of any kind. I was exhausted, and in no way looking for sex. I simply wanted to feel close to her, but my gesture was met with repulsion. Already riddled with self-doubt, her rejection was the last thing I needed. For years, I'd felt that no matter where we were, or what we were doing, everything about me irritated her. That final repudiation caused me to lose my temper resulting in a moment that I have always regretted handling the way I did.

I told her to get out of my bed, and to get out of my apartment. Her company was paying for her hotel, so I figured she could stay there for the rest of her time in the city. I was done. Done being pushed away, and feeling guilty for wanting to be close to her. Done tiptoeing around trying not to upset her in anyway.

In the past, I'd tried to communicate, and get her to tell me what was going on, but she denied any issues and would quickly change the subject. But now, I was finally standing up for myself and taking control of the moment as well as my own feelings. There would be no more sitting back trying to avoid confrontation. Our relationship wasn't working, and I'd had enough.

When she returned to Toronto, we spoke on the phone and agreed that a separation was inevitable, but as my contract with *Evita* was coming to an end, we began to argue more aggressively about the logistics. The upcoming season at Stratford was something that our girls were excited about, but unless we managed to come to some agreements, my wife was quite content to have them pulled from the show.

In order to deal with my home life, I was forced to leave *Evita* early and travel back to Toronto. Leaving a show like that was something I'd never had to do before, and while the whole situation left me feeling humiliated and defeated, I hoped it wouldn't leave too much of a stain on my reputation.

By this point, I was experiencing anxiety attacks on a daily basis, and I soon realized that I needed to get my shit together. Christ, I thought. I've got leads at Stratford next season. I backed off the drinking, and had my medication increased to help deal with my worsening depressive state.

At home, things showed no signs of calming down. My wife was furious at the idea that I now wanted a divorce, and fought me at every turn. I couldn't understand why she would want to stay in a marriage that she clearly didn't want to be in.

Over time, we were able to have some rational conversations during which it was made clear to me that we needed to be away from each other, and my upcoming season at Stratford was the perfect opportunity. After some pleading, I managed to convince her that having our daughters in the show would be a wonderful experience for them, and although we'd be in Stratford, she could come visit them anytime she wanted.

Originally, it was supposed to be just my daughters and myself moving to Stratford, until the nanny that my wife hired the year before asked me to take her with us. She loved our girls, and still wanted the opportunity to take care of them, so I decided to bring her along.

This turned out to be helpful in the end, since sometimes after a show, when the girls were tired, I'd need to take them home right away. And with the nanny there to watch them, I was able to meet up with cast members for the odd post-show drink down the street which often resulted in me having to be driven home.

13

KNOWING WHEN TO LEAVE

As the grandfather clock chimed for quarter past three, my mum got up from her chair and walked to the kitchen window. She stared out for a moment at a solitary hummingbird eating from the feeder hanging from the crabapple tree in the backyard.

"These are for me?" I asked, noticing the tissue wrapped china plates separated to one end of the box by a cardboard barrier.

Turning from the window to engage, she said, "I figured that you might want those."

She knew full well that I did.

My mum loved musicals, and had been a big fan of *The King and I* and Yul Brynner ever since my sister and I had done the show in the 1980s. It's no surprise that she'd have a set of commemorative plates from the film. The story, based on the 1944 novel *Anna and the King of Siam,* by Margaret Landon, follows Anna Leonowens while she is governess to the children of King Mongkut of Siam in the early 1860s.

Twenty years after my theatrical debut, I found myself back in the show that started it all, only this time, at the prestigious Stratford Festival of Canada. Playing the romantic lead role of Lun Tha, I felt I had come full circle with *The King and I,* only this time

I had an added connection to the show since both my daughters were appearing as royal children.

Watching the show each night from the wings filled me with a sense of gratitude. It wasn't just that my girls were given such an amazing opportunity, but that I got the chance to spend that year bonding with them through moments that would be unequivocally the best of my life.

That season at Stratford, presented a rare opportunity to have real visibility in Canadian theatre. Shakespeare's *The Adventures of Pericles* was being cross-cast with company members from *The King and I,* which meant that a large portion of the cast would be actors of colour. The director had developed a great concept for the show, and the cast felt involved in the process of creating the piece.

It was my first lead role in a Shakespeare play, and it was important for me to have people of colour see themselves represented in that specific genre of theatre. Growing up, I never really saw anyone who looked like me doing Shakespeare, so I never thought that it would be something I could achieve.

Although I was nervous about the language at first, one of my acting coaches put me at ease when he told me to trust my instincts, and that as long as I understood what I was saying, the audience would understand.

I played King Simonides, the father of Thaisa whose hand in marriage is won by Pericles in a tournament of knights. I used my own experiences as a father to help me with the character, and I was especially proud to have my daughters watch me in the show. It was challenging, but it solidified my position as an "actor" at Stratford.

I felt very much at home on the Festival Theatre stage, and surprisingly, even more so with Shakespeare, but my anxiety was still a huge issue for me during the season. Even though I felt in control of my emotions for the most part, I think my attacks were made worse by problems I was still having at home.

The situation with my wife was becoming more and more difficult to navigate. I'd set up a bedroom in my house in Stratford where she would stay on weekends while visiting the girls. The arrangement made our separation a little awkward, but I eventually accepted that it was the best solution. As hard as it was for me, I could see my wife struggle to keep a connection with our daughters as she watched them enjoy being part of something that she could neither appreciate nor understand. Nevertheless, the time my wife and I spent apart was extremely beneficial, and even though things had been difficult for us, I still held out hope that we would eventually work things out.

My parents knew about my separation, but never really pressed me on the issue. There was really no way to know how they felt about it, because anytime I mentioned it, they didn't really have anything to say. My mum had been a great listener though, which I always appreciated. Even if she couldn't offer any insight into what I should do, she always allowed me to vent. I didn't care to be honest, because sometimes just being able to say things out loud helped me put things into perspective.

When they came to see a matinee performance of *The King and I*, my parents stayed for my youngest daughter's birthday party. It was nice to see them spending time with their granddaughters. I think that hearing those songs again, while watching them onstage, brought back memories of seeing me in the same show when I was a child. They also saw the show a second time when they came near the end of the season for my oldest daughter's birthday. My parents loved when I would work at Stratford because it was much closer for them to come and visit.

The truth of the matter was, being busy and living further away hadn't been the only reasons we didn't see them. I still couldn't let go of my mother's past assertions that I wasn't raising my kids with enough stability. This made it uncomfortable for me to have my parents around, especially as my daughters got older. But the more I saw how much they adored my girls, the more I began to rethink how I felt.

My wife and I continued our separation but during her visits we attempted to communicate what we wanted out of the relationship. We were slowly reconnecting in a way we hadn't for quite some time, and my daughters seemed mostly unaffected through it all. My drinking was getting under control, and I was starting to feel like I was going to be okay despite the uncertainty of the future with my wife. I think what kept me on the right track was that extraordinary experience of being able to engage with my daughters by bringing them into a small part of my world.

On leaving Stratford at the end of the season, my wife and I decided to give our marriage another chance, which ended up quite embarrassingly short-lived. After about three days at home, my wife turned to me in bed, took a deep breath, and proceeded to ask me where I saw myself in the future. It was her passive-aggressive way of asking if I had any job prospects. I had been unemployed for a hot second, and for the first time in my long career, really didn't have anything on the horizon because I was exhausted and not really looking.

Something came to mind in that moment. Something that she had said to me not too long after we'd met. I'd been extremely tired at the end of a week of shows during *Miss Saigon* in Toronto, when she told me she couldn't understand why. She said, "All you do is go...la la la for a few hours a night." At the time, I thought she was kidding, but I'd now come to realize that she actually meant it. Remembering that comment helped me finally understand the root cause of many of our relationship problems: the lack of respect for my career and thusly, a lack of respect for me.

Perhaps she resented me for being able to do what I loved to do for a living. Maybe because to her it didn't look like work, she felt it wasn't. She, on the other hand, had been working hard to climb the corporate ladder in the financial industry in order to make as much money as she could, all the while, hating her job.

There could be no relationship without mutual respect, and so I knew our marriage needed to end. The sooner I got out, the better it would be for all involved, and although I ended up staying for a while longer in a clichéd excuse of "it's for the kids," I was actively looking for a way out.

She certainly knew it was over, and admitted as much to me. It was just a matter of time before I worked out the logistics. For years I hadn't felt that I was an equal partner in our relationship, but once I made it official, there would be no turning back.

As difficult as it was going to be, I was confident that it was what was best not only for me, but especially for my daughters. It would benefit them to live in two separate happy homes, instead of a single miserable one filled with resentment. It was the right decision, but one that broke my heart. I loved my wife deeply for many years, and it was sad to think I would never get that feeling back.

By the time I was finally ready to look for work, I received a call about an audition for the Toronto theatre company, CanStage. They were mounting a little-known show called *Urinetown* as part of their upcoming 2004 season, and as it is with most contemporary not-for-profit theatre, it was only scheduled for a limited run of approximately six weeks.

I had declined auditioning for the show when the notices first went out, feeling I wasn't ready to go back to work so soon, but I was being called in because they were looking for one more character that they thought I would be right for.

Of course…shocker! It was the only character of colour. I really wasn't up to playing another seemingly tokenized role, but with the state of my marriage and the fact that I needed a job, I decided to go in to audition for the creative team anyway.

Later that same day, I was cast in the role of Billy Boy Bill, in *Urinetown's* Canadian premiere. My decision to take the contract stirred up a real mix of emotions. I wanted more free time with my daughters, but I was happy to have work in town. In the end, the new gig ended up a welcome distraction from how I'd been feeling about the end of my marriage.

Urinetown started as a relatively obscure off-Broadway musical about a time when the depletion of the Earth's natural resources has caused the water table to drop significantly. In this satirical comedy, this one particular community does away with private toilets in homes, and instead, citizens are required to use pay toilets in an effort to conserve water. After making its way to Broadway, the show took everyone by surprise by being nominated for ten Tony Awards, and winning three. Best book of a musical, best original score, and best direction.

We were going to be working with the original director and choreographer, so I was excited to dive into rehearsals. Slightly distracted by things at home, I still managed to keep my focus on the task at hand. As the dance captain and assistant to the choreographer, I was taking on extra responsibility which I gladly welcomed.

Simply through word of mouth, *Urinetown* became the "little show that could." The performances kept extending as we watched bigger shows close all around us. New productions of *Hairspray* and *The Producers* closed months ahead of schedule, as well as *Mamma Mia.* The show was a huge success, and our cast just continued to enjoy the ride.

Up until that point in my career, my parents had managed to see almost everything I was in once, but my mum loved this show so much she made sure to come back a second time. I hadn't seen them in a few months, and they were somehow looking a lot older than I'd remembered. *Urinetown* was really up their ally, since they'd always seemed to enjoy comedy and satire much more than the dramatic epic musicals I'd often appeared in. I really appreciated that they saw the show more than once. It was a testament to the work we were doing, and since we were really pushing for ticket sales, I felt that I really had their support.

Midway through our extremely successful run, I received a call from my sister asking for help dealing with the Children's Aid Society and her search for our biological father. She'd submitted her request, but hadn't heard anything for quite some time, so I thought I'd reach out to the social worker who'd helped me. Since the search for our biological mother had turned up nothing, both my sister and I were convinced that it would be the same with the search for our father.

The worker that I'd dealt with from CAS explained that since it wasn't her case, she couldn't really give me any details about my sister's search without her permission, and understandably so. She did however ask her colleague in charge to give my sister an update. Later that same day I heard back from my worker who informed me that she had just finished talking to my biological grandmother on the phone.

I was shocked. How did we go from no information in the morning, to talking to our biological father's family in the afternoon? As the worker explained to me, she opened the file and there was a phone number in St. Louis, Missouri, for a contact person. The worker called the number, and my biological father's mother, my grandmother, answered the phone in the apartment she'd lived in for over fifty years.

It was a sudden and exciting piece of news that my sister and I really didn't expect. In all honesty, I think we'd put these searches behind us, having felt we'd reconciled our past and moved on. But no matter. We gave permission for everyone to swap phone numbers, and eventually, I ended up talking to my biological grandmother on the phone.

As one would expect, it was an emotionally charged interaction. She sounded lovely and was so filled with joy over finding us that she could barely speak from crying. A lump was in my throat as well, and although I couldn't remember who this woman was, she remembered me, and that meant everything.

How to tell my parents of our latest discovery was a delicate endeavour, and one that I'd been nervous about for quite some time. Finding a birth sibling is one thing, but a parent is something else altogether.

Both my sister and I knew that if we were ever to meet one or both of our biological parents, it might be difficult to tell our adoptive parents. We didn't want to offend them in any way, and we worried that they'd feel abandoned if we felt a connection to the people who shared our DNA. I was pretty confident that wouldn't be the case with us, since we'd been through something similar before.

When my adoptive mother was eighteen, she became pregnant, and realizing that she wasn't ready to be a mother, she'd given up the child for adoption. I'd known very little about the circumstances surrounding the situation, but knew that it had been a heartbreaking decision for her. It may have been something that fed her desire to adopt us when she felt ready, and a contributing factor in the constant confrontations she and I had throughout my childhood.

My mum and the son she'd given up had been reunited while I was doing *Miss Saigon* in Toronto, and unfortunately, the relationship he was looking for wasn't one my mum was prepared to have. Both his adoptive parents had died, and he was looking to my mother to fill the void they'd left behind. My mum was interested in getting to know him, but not to the extent that she'd replace the mother that raised him. It didn't take long for the relationship to simply fizzle out, until eventually, we never really heard from him again.

When my sister and I told my parents about our biological father, they seemed genuinely happy for us, although, I think my mum was secretly relieved that it wasn't our biological mother. I'd tried to reassure my dad that nobody would take his place, even though he constantly informed us that he felt completely fine about everything. My dad appeared stoic, but I could see for the first time that he was not quite as self-assured as he normally liked to project.

When my sister and I decided to take the trip out to St. Louis to meet our family for the first time, I understood from my mum's experience that it had the potential to be an emotionally complicated misadventure. Although things were not great between us, and I was waiting for the right time to leave, my wife insisted on going with me, while making it clear that she didn't understand why I needed to take the trip in the first place. This added an extra layer of stress to the situation.

This was one of the most important things to happen to me, and the person I'd shared my life with for almost ten years seemed unmoved. Her true feelings became clear as my hurt turned to sadness and my sadness to anger. And when all was said and done, I knew I'd never look at her the same way again.

When meeting my biological father and his family, I decided not to let my wife's attitude ruin the intensely delicate moment. As a result, I had a wonderful time meeting everyone although it was a bit surreal to look at my birth father and see myself looking back at me. I discovered that I was the fourth of my name, and that he was referred to as Junior to avoid any confusion with his father. He had two sisters that welcomed us, as well as my grandmother and a cousin. Both my aunts looked at least fifteen years younger than they actually were, which excited my sister since she resembled the younger of the two. Unfortunately for me, the same could not be said about my father, and once we dispensed with the usual pleasantries, I looked him up and down and immediately launched into my first question: "How much of this is self-induced, and how much of this do I have to look forward to?" He laughed, and freely admitted that I had nothing to worry about. Most of it was a result of some pretty fast and hard living. I'm assuming he was referring to all of his travelling days as a blues guitarist in the sixties and seventies. The trouble was, he couldn't remember much, which I came to understand was proof that he'd actually lived in the moment.

At his apartment in a low-income housing development, he didn't appear to have many belongings. It was late summer, and because it was so hot, the inside of the apartment was dimly lit and there was a small fan to keep the place cool. There were minimal furnishings, all mid-century, but none of it was coordinated in any way.

I noticed his guitars which were placed on stands around the room, and when he asked if I knew how to play, I was excited to let him know that I did. I pointed out that we were both self-taught, although he was taken under the wing of a blues legend and Hall of Famer when he was only fifteen years old.

The two of us had the chance to jam a little, and even though blues wasn't really my thing, I managed to keep up with him just the same. My sister made an interesting nature versus nurture observation, that both he and I had identical ways of holding our guitars, which everyone thought was uncanny.

The mood wasn't always light, and when I got the chance to be alone with him, Junior opened up to me about my abandonment and eventual adoption. He confided in me that the one and only time he'd been to Canada, he'd played a blues festival in Ottawa which is where he met my mother after one of his shows. They spent the week together, and even though he wasn't looking for anything serious, she hopped on the band's bus and followed him home to St. Louis with nothing but the clothes on her back.

The relationship was doomed from the start, and after I was born, it became more and more apparent that things were never going to work out. At one point, a few weeks after my sister was born, things took a violent turn and a physical altercation ensued. The police were called to remove us from the home, and my mother was placed on a plane back to Canada with my sister and me in tow. We never saw my father again.

After we were eventually abandoned and sent to foster care, the CAS reached out to our father's family. Our grandmother then worked with them to have us returned into her care, and they agreed with the stipulation that our father had no further contact with us. This condition, I assumed was because of the past abuse allegations.

When social services did their home visit with my grandmother at her apartment in St. Louis, my father showed up there. As a result, the CAS rescinded their offer to release us into my grandmother's care, and my sister and I would remain in the Canadian foster system for the next few years until we were adopted. Although this wasn't the story I had hoped for, I am grateful that I got a bit of closure, and a chance to know a little bit more of what led to my adoption.

The meeting with my family was an overall good experience, and even after learning some of my birth father's history, I decided to keep an open mind. After all, I was the last person who should be judging someone by the actions of their past. Having only known him a short while, I got the sense that he'd either grown into a different person, or at the very least had learned how to move forward.

At the end of our visit, my sister and I became more emotional than either of us had anticipated. I can't speak for her but for me, it was difficult, partially because I knew in the back of my mind I probably wouldn't see him or his family much after that. I wanted to make sure we kept in touch, but it was impossible to know when I'd be able to make that trip again.

I returned home heartbroken, not just because the visit was so short, but because taking that trip with my wife led me to the decision that it was time for me to finally leave her. When I told her, she pleaded with me to get marriage counselling, which was something I had begged her for in the past, but my efforts were always dismissed because she felt that we didn't have a problem. This may have been true for her, but the fact that I was unhappy would indicate that there were definitely some issues. As a result, I was forced to shut down emotionally just to be able to live and function in the same house. I despised what our relationship had become and because I'd been so hurt, I was tired of trying to make it work.

I knew that the situation wasn't easy for my wife and it caused a rift between her and her family when her sister had suggested that our daughters should live with me. Fortunately, my wife and I had always been on the same page when it came to the girls. There was no question that we'd have joint custody, and even though my wife's home would be their primary residence, there was never any issue.

Shortly after our split, I received notice that *Urinetown* was closing, and I was suddenly in the difficult position of having to look for work again. The stress of unemployment coupled with the finality of my marriage, pushed me into another anxiety-riddled depression that I wasn't entirely sure I'd be able come back from.

14

LOOKIN' GOOD, BUT FEELIN' BAD

"I noticed that there's no other show programs in the box," I mentioned to my mum. "I guess you didn't see me in anything after *Urinetown.*"

"You never really asked us to," she responded. "I know you did that show with the country singer, but you never let us know about anything else."

"There wasn't anything worth seeing me in, if I'm honest."

Those were dark and difficult times for me. I wish I'd have been able to talk to my mum a bit more, and let her know everything that was going on in my life, but a huge part of me was embarrassed when it came to my many shortcomings.

I managed to secure another contract with CanStage and their production of *Ain't Misbehavin'*, the Tony Award-winning musical revue and tribute to the music of Fats Waller. I went into the show as a swing, covering the two male roles, and as expected, it was a lot of work. Rehearsals started shortly after the closing of *Urinetown,* which gave me a little time to move into the house I'd purchased in downtown Toronto.

It wasn't until I was finally settled into my new home and the separation papers were signed that things went horribly wrong.

Since she decided to keep the house we shared in the suburbs, my wife bought me out of my interest and re-mortgaged. I purchased my new house with the buyout, and was still able to have a small nest egg left over in case of gaps between gigs.

Not long after I closed on my house, my entire savings had been removed from my bank account. I was told by the bank that it was to cover my portion of the debts we'd incurred as a married couple, even though according to our separation agreement, those had been dealt with by the lawyers in the transfer of the house. This was clearly a mistake. One that would take over two years to rectify.

Now I was left without a safety net and feeling completely defeated. Once again, in order to cope, I turned to the warm embrace of pills and alcohol. I felt unable to dig myself out of the hole I was in, so I just continued to simply drown my sorrows.

I spoke to my mum about things only a handful of times, and I found her to be surprisingly comforting. I was reminded of the time I'd run away as a child and how she had warmed me up with a bowl of tomato soup. Perhaps she'd recognized my pain and instinctively knew the right words I needed to hear.

Having lost everything, I fell into the darkest place I'd ever been as my anxiety flew into overdrive. I started drinking so heavily that I wasn't even able to remember anything about my time in *Ain't Misbehavin'*. Being the understudy for the two male lead roles, I was needed only in emergency situations and therefore wasn't on for most performances. This made it easy to show up drunk to work and not really have anyone notice. Even though I'd gone on at least twice for one of the roles I covered, I had no real recollection of what I did. Normally I could remember lyrics, harmonies, and even choreography years after a show, but for that one, I remembered little to nothing.

My drinking had become so out of control that I often felt I needed it just to get through the day. At night, when I had difficulty sleeping, I'd mix my anxiety medication into my drink as a kind of sleepy-time cocktail to ease me into a state of unconsciousness where I'd come to find life more favourable.

When the show closed early, I found myself with no work and not enough money to cover my expenses. I started falling behind on my car and mortgage payments as things started to spiral out of control.

There were times in my life when I'd felt that virtually everything was going wrong, but my experiences during that dark period were next level. My answering machine was constantly full, not with job offers, but with collection agency messages that displayed a clear indication of their unfamiliarity with the analogy of getting blood from a stone.

After a Sunday matinee performance, I returned home to find several phone messages. One in particular was rather peculiar, and though not from a collector, it was nonetheless distressing. It was from a friend of mine in the UK who had left it on my machine for my ex-wife, which was strange enough, but she seemed shocked and surprised when it was me who returned her call. She had read someone's inquiry about a memorial service for me on a *Miss Saigon* fansite where someone mistakenly assumed that I'd passed away. I wasn't entirely sure why someone would think I was dead. I mean, my career had stalled a little, but not enough to warrant that kind of assumption.

As it happened, another actor who looked like me had committed suicide, and my guess was that a fan had confused the two of us. In retrospect, it was kind of people to inquire about my "celebration of life," but this misidentification couldn't have come at a worse time, especially considering everything else I had been going through. Eventually, I was able to clear everything up, which provided some relief to my family, as well as to my friend who had alerted me to the initial mistake.

My parents were happy to know that the misunderstanding about my demise had been resolved, and they offered some suggestions about getting my finances in order and moving forward with my life. The situation had left me far too overwhelmed to comprehend a way to fix things, and although they knew that I was in dire straits, they never once offered any financial help. Not that I would have accepted it mind you. It just would have been nice for them to ask. I tried not to be too upset, but when I discovered that they'd loaned my older sister and her husband tens of thousands of dollars over the years, I was a little put out. Not surprised, but definitely put out.

I wasn't going to let it get to me. After all, I'd been in this very situation before, so why was this any different? Left feeling alone without any real support system, I found it too difficult to resist the comfort I'd come to know in the warmth of vodka's sweet kiss.

When *Ain't Misbehavin'* closed, I was lucky enough to have booked a concert version of *Annie Get Your Gun* at Massey Hall, but two weeks prior to rehearsals, the male lead dropped out of the show, putting it in jeopardy.

Not quite sure of our fate, I continued to self-destruct, sleeping all day and drinking to the point of blacking out. I wasn't eating properly or taking care of myself, and it would often be days before I even found the urge to shower.

Finally, in an enormous stroke of luck, a famous country music recording artist, and mullet aficionado, agreed to step into the role, and we forged ahead with the show. I had no way of knowing whether I'd be able to hide my issues from the rest of the company, because as a drunk, I wasn't overly self-aware. Even if they noticed that I wasn't in a particularly good place, I didn't think at the time that anyone suspected the magnitude of what'd I'd been going through. That may have changed, however, after I lost my house, and was forced to start selling off my belongings.

The cast must have known something serious was going on when I started trying to sell my framed show posters and other memorabilia at work. As could be expected, there wasn't much interest in purchasing the remnants of a career that was slowly crumbling with each and every drink. So instead, I packed the majority of my things in boxes suitable for future eBay transactions.

Once the show closed and my house was gone, I was left homeless for the second time in my life, although this time, at least I could sleep in my car while I tried to sort myself out. Most devastating was that without a home, I wasn't able to spend time with my daughters. There were a couple of weekends where I'd been a deadbeat dad for not picking them up, but the truth was I had nowhere to go, and no means to feed or entertain them. I was too terribly embarrassed to say anything about my situation, and I couldn't see what purpose telling them would serve.

My sister offered me a place to stay until I could get back on my feet, which I hoped wouldn't take too long since I'd been offered a role in *Oklahoma*, at Theatre Aquarius in Hamilton. The show wouldn't start rehearsals for a number of weeks, so my intention was to stay with her until I could rent a place of my own.

My sister's house was a welcome change, and I was starting to feel a little bit better. I had a roof over my head, and my sister was an amazing support system giving me confidence that things would eventually turn around.

I seemed to be doing much better just prior to rehearsals until the day I'd tried to refill the prescription for my anxiety meds, and the pharmacy informed me that my insurance had been cancelled.

The drugs were expensive, and I had no way of paying for them. As a result, I started rationing what I had left, and drinking more to take the edge off. I was reaching the end of my rope, and the levels of stress and anxiety I'd been under were more than I could handle.

I woke up one morning completely out of it after having washed down some of my meds with a bottom shelf vodka the night before. This landed me in the hospital and having to quit the show. I blamed everyone around me but myself. By this time, I felt I'd lost everything. Not just my house and car, but any credibility I had as an actor. Money had never been that important to me, but now, because I didn't have any, I could feel my ability to be a good father to my daughters slipping away. They were the most important part of my life, and I was losing them fast.

I moved out of my sister's house and went back to Toronto, where I stayed with my agent who was kind enough to take me in. Still, I felt I'd reached the end of the road, and was simply biding my time until I inevitably drank myself to death.

Because of the prescription coverage debacle, my lawyer, who I'd retained with what little money I had left, met me in court for an expedited case conference in my divorce proceedings. Because of the painful withdrawal I was going through, my ex-wife's sudden and premature cancellation of my prescription coverage was the main focus that day. The judge ultimately sorted things so that I could begin to get my life back on track.

As a way of getting me back on my feet, my agent managed to negotiate a contract with Disney Cruise Line, which not only provided a decent income, but a chance to distance myself from the stressors that were constantly gnawing away at me at home. I struggled with the decision to take the contract, knowing that not only would I be away from my daughters, but I was afraid my ex would find some way to use my absence against me. The decision to accept was finally made out of pure desperation to make some money, since the legal costs for the divorce which had yet to be finalized, were continuing to add up. At least this way, I'd be able to finance each individual legal battle, not to mention pay down some of my debts.

The saving grace was that the eight weeks of rehearsal for the cruise were done at a studio in downtown Toronto. During that time, I was provided with my own one-bedroom condominium, where I could have my daughters stay on weekends. Not that I didn't appreciate living with my agent, but I'd already overstayed my welcome, and didn't want to burden her further. I was feeling a new sense of hope, and managed to stay sober while I started my job with Disney. This helped me focus not just on work, but on the relationship with my daughters.

During rehearsals, a friend had introduced me to a lawyer who thought he could help with the banking error that had led to my current state. He was new to the law society, and looking for new cases, so in return for representing me, he asked only for court filing costs. His plan was to deal with the issue head on, and although suing the bank directly seemed like a long shot, he was right. The lawsuit set in motion a chain of events which allowed me to recoup my lost funds while at the same time finally settling my divorce.

I was relieved at the finality of things, and for the duration of my Disney contract, I kept busy as I counted down the days till I could go home and see my daughters.

Back in Toronto, I moved in with a girlfriend with whom I'd rekindled a romance with while on a break from the ship. We'd been friends for a while when I was still together with my wife, and I often turned to her when I needed someone to talk to. She also appreciated having someone to vent to, seeing as she too had gone through a breakup and was pregnant when we met. Several months after leaving my wife, my friend and I became romantically involved for a short time, but it ended poorly most likely because it was too soon for me. Not fully healed from the aftermath of my failed marriage, my self-esteem had gone into hiding along with my dignity, and I found it too difficult to deal with her terrible temper.

Always an optimist, I held out hope that this girlfriend had changed, but it didn't take long for her to show her true colours. While things started out okay, her mood swung hard, and so did her fists. I tolerated her behaviour for a little while out of concern for her two-year-old son, but her verbal and physical abuse became too much to handle.

After a few months, things took a terrible, but not unexpected turn for the worse. I'd always known her temper to run a little hot, but it soon reached levels I had never anticipated. In preparation for a job interview, I was up late one evening working on my resumé. Expecting a long night, I had just made a fresh pot of coffee when I suddenly found myself in the middle of an argument. It was over something ridiculously minor, which was pretty much on brand for us as a couple, but when the exchange became exceedingly heated, she picked up the boiling coffee, and threw it on me.

The pain was worse than anything I'd ever experienced, so my tears and screams of agony were well warranted. After some difficulty trying to remove my shirt, I was able to discard it and focus enough on finding my way to the front door. Distracted by the searing pain, I struggled to find the car keys, but once I had them, I stumbled to the car, and drove off to her parents' home. Letting myself in with a spare key, I didn't hesitate to wake them. They immediately drove me to the hospital, where I was treated for second-degree burns to my arms, head, and neck. I stayed with her parents for a while, and they tended to me and helped me change the dressings on my burns. They were sane people with perspective, and they advised me to leave her. But like some made-for-TV movie of the week, at the point when I should have run for the hills, I accepted her apology, and her promise not to lose her temper again, which didn't last very long.

A few weeks later, she and I faced off again, but this time while my daughters were visiting. I tried never to argue in front of my girls because they'd seen enough of that when their mother and I were together. Naturally I felt terrible that I was exposing them to another domestic altercation. This time I was pushed down a flight of stairs, and kicked repeatedly, while my oldest daughter, terrified by what was happening, put in a call to 911.

Once officers arrived on the scene, they were of course bombarded with stories of how I'd been the aggressor, but with both my daughters as witnesses, there was little doubt who was at fault, and my newly minted ex-girlfriend was arrested. She was eventually charged with two counts of assault, one for that evening's performance and the other for my second-degree burns which police discovered during the course of their investigation.

I never forgave myself for exposing my daughters to so much unpleasantness, but what I did learn about toxic relationships, was that "I love you," can be the most abusive words when they come from someone who consistently hurts you.

Amidst all that turmoil, Disney offered me another contract aboard another one of their ships, which meant I'd have the opportunity to shift my focus elsewhere and leave the relationship drama behind.

"Mum, do you remember that girlfriend of mine with the little boy?"

My mother sat very still in her chair, staring as though she was looking right through me. She didn't answer right away.

"Mum," I said. "Did you hear me?"

Snapping back to reality, she said, "I knew that relationship would end badly."

"Thanks Mum, I wish you'd said something before I had to go through all that shit with her."

"You never would have listened anyway."

She was right. I never would have listened to her opinion on the matter, even if she'd offered it.

15

I AM WHAT I AM

After a second fairly straightforward contract at sea, I was ready to head home again. With my divorce now final, I had the chance to reinvent myself, though I was tentative about where to begin. I had no home, not much savings and although I felt that I was still on the downswing of my career, my drinking was under control, and I was slowly starting to realize that even though I was alone, I was going to be okay.

The decision to leave my acting career, though bittersweet, was ultimately not a difficult one to make. Theatre had been my life, it's what fed my soul and gave me much of my identity. It also fed my insecurities, often fuelling my anxiety, and causing stress.

At the same time, my daughters, the indisputable loves of my life, were the most important part of my existence. In the end, the choice was very simple. If I was going to be any kind of a father at all, I needed to be at home, where I'd be close to them. And since theatre in Toronto had slowed down significantly over the past several years, I would also need to find a way to make a regular paycheque.

Going back to school was inevitable since I wanted a new career and not just a job. Remembering that at one time I'd considered becoming a nurse, I realized I hadn't lost my passion to help others. I knew that I would be happy finding a career in healthcare, and since time was also an influencing factor, I decided on a two-year diploma program in massage therapy. Having benefitted so much from it when I was performing, massage seemed a perfect match for me. I registered for school, and moved myself to a suburb just west of Toronto where my daughters and my ex were living with her new boyfriend.

My Disney contract left me with some money, but in order to furnish a new apartment for myself and my daughters, I was going to need a bit of help. My worst fear had been realized, and although I had to swallow every ounce of pride I had left, I decided to ask my parents for a loan. A few thousand dollars would help me with my rent and utilities while getting settled into my course at school. Having to ask them took everything out of me. I prided myself with never having to ask them for help, and here I was with no other option.

I couldn't wrap my head around the fact that I even had to ask. If one of my daughters was going through anything close to what I'd been through, I wouldn't hesitate to ask how I could help. Even with limited financial resources, I would find some way, because that's what you do for family.

It took a few days for my parents to process my loan application, and when they did, the approval came with a small lecture on fiscal responsibility, as well as a monthly spreadsheet on how much was left to pay on both the principal and interest. Yes, interest! Apparently, this was the same deal that both of my sisters had been offered when they received help from my parents over the years. Feeling the sting of the salt in my wounds, I sucked it up, and took the loan. The faster I could get through school, the better.

I also secured a student loan but the exorbitant cost of tuition and books forced me to take a job in a restaurant as a dishwasher in order to help make ends meet. Working full-time hours while going to school was extremely difficult to manage, but finding help at a local addiction facility and the idea of a normal life with my daughters helped to keep me focused.

As excited as I was to be starting with new things, I was preparing to have closure on some old ones. My ex-girlfriend, the coffee connoisseur and domestic abuse enthusiast, had her trial coming up, and I was nervous about seeing her again. My sister came to the courthouse for moral support, which I appreciated, and although I thought I wouldn't be able to go through with it, she convinced me that I was doing the right thing.

It didn't actually take that long. I testified and it ultimately came down to her word against mine. Interestingly, when the judge made her ruling, she indicated that there was no doubt in her mind that my ex-girlfriend had done the things she was accused of, but unfortunately, the Crown couldn't meet its burden of proof.

The outcome was disappointing. Still, I took comfort in the fact that not only did she have the embarrassment of being arrested twice, but those arrests would always stay on her record. Despite being acquitted, what she'd done would follow her for the rest of her life.

At the end of that year, my oldest daughter was preparing to graduate from the eighth grade. Time was flying by so quickly, and I couldn't believe how fast she'd grown into a young lady. Since I had an extremely limited budget, I went to a thrift store to find a suit, and after a fairly adequate hemming job, I was all set to go to the ceremony.

Afterwards, the students and parents were invited for a lovely mother/son or father/daughter dance, but when the music started, and I looked around, there was no sign of my daughter. When I finally spotted her across the gymnasium, I saw that she was dancing with her mother's boyfriend while her mother took pictures. My heart fell into my shoes. I thought that we would have had a beautiful moment to share, but it was being shared with someone else.

She then saw me from the other side of the gym and came over so we could dance, but sadly, after only a few steps, the song had finished. I managed to hold back my tears as she explained to me that her mother told her to dance with the boyfriend.

I completely understood. Of course my daughter would want to appease everyone, that's still who she is. After all, this man was in her life too. My daughter's beautiful heart, was definitely in the right place, but at the time, I couldn't help feeling hurt. Smiling, I kissed her, congratulated her, and left her to enjoy the rest of her school dance.

After making my way home, I curled up in front of the television with a tub of ice cream and cried for about an hour. God how I wanted a drink, but after all the work I'd put in at AA, I knew that for the sake of my girls, that was something I could never go back to.

Things became easier as my schooling came closer to an end, and at thirty-eight, having passed all my board exams, I found myself embarking on my new career as a registered massage therapist.

By now, my oldest daughter was enjoying high school, making new friends, and focusing on her studies. My youngest, who was in the eighth grade, and usually focused on academics, had found a new love of basketball, and was on the school team. I was lucky enough to make my own hours at work which meant I was able to attend all the games.

On the surface, it seemed that everyone was alright and adjusting to a somewhat normal life, but in my ex's household, that couldn't have been further from the truth. While I idled in her driveway on a Friday afternoon, waiting to take my daughters for the weekend, my ex-wife came out to talk to me, which wasn't normal by any stretch of the imagination. The walk from her front door to my car was eerily long, and left me afraid of what was to come.

She was fairly calm and actually somewhat pleasant as she explained to me that my youngest daughter was going to have to come and live with me. Apparently, she had been acting up, and her behavior was too "disruptive" to my ex-wife's household. At twelve years old, my youngest was having to deal with a shitload of sudden changes in her life. There was a new man living in the house, as well as the anticipated arrival of her mother's new baby.

The problems had been ongoing, but they were made worse about a month prior to my ex's due date, when she decided to give our daughters each a memory box. Inside were old photos of us as a family, and a gift of our old wedding rings, hers for my oldest, and mine, which years earlier I had presumed was lost, was given to my youngest. There were letters that outlined how the boxes contained the past, and how with a new baby, they needed to move forward with their new family and a bright new future. I'm not really sure how it was intended, but my twelve-year-old daughter interpreted it to mean: forget about your dad and let's move on with a new life. It was so upsetting for her that I was called to pick her up from school that day because she'd been inconsolable.

I was quite happy to have my youngest come live with me, and I did my best to help her through the extremely difficult situation of being so dispassionately uprooted from her home. My ex-wife had decided to put some distance between the two of them because she feared that our daughter would be angry with her. An accurate assessment indeed, although not overly clairvoyant.

A lot of changes were happening in a short period of time, and since I'd only just begun my massage career, things were difficult for me financially. Unsurprisingly, as I sat and listened to my ex tell me how having my youngest live with me would be the best thing for her, she made very sure to tell me that since her and her boyfriend were also "struggling" financially, she couldn't offer any support in that department.

The revelation of her financial stress couldn't have been more perfectly timed. As if out of some comedy sketch show, at the very moment she was expressing her financial woes, I literally watched a mini excavator make its way into her backyard to start digging out her new salt-water pool.

"I feel terrible," I told her. "I was unaware just how bad things had been for you." To be fair, being without a pool in her neighborhood would more than likely have made her a social pariah. I decided to let it go, because if I'd learned anything about dealing with my ex-wife, it was to pick my battles.

Once my youngest moved in with me, her and I butted heads for the first little while, and it didn't take a psychologist to figure out why. She was angry at her mother and taking it out on the closest person to her, which happened to be me. When I was finally able to really talk to her, she cried in my arms and asked me, "Why doesn't my mother love me like you love me?" I tried to be strong in that moment, but my heart was completely shattered. It was as though I was reliving everything that I'd been through when I was her age. How I'd felt unloved and unwanted by those who were supposed to protect me.

The hardest thing for a parent is to watch their child in pain, and so I tried my best to explain that her mother *did* love her, but had her own way of showing it.

My daughter had been completely uprooted, but despite it all, she persevered. I laid down some ground rules, but nothing too drastic since I felt it would be unfair to put her through too much change.

As a parent, I tried my best to listen, and make sure that *both* my daughters knew they were heard, even if I didn't always agree with what they had to say. In order to never minimize their feelings, I found it much easier to put myself in their world rather than insist that they come into mine. This was something I wished my parents would have been able to do when I was a kid.

Counselling was also important in helping me deal with any issues that would arise. I like to think that I provided the right environment for my daughter to thrive, and I was extremely proud of how she learned to handle herself despite the situation. She had worked through a lot of difficult emotions and went on to have an extremely successful year at school. Seeing this, my ex decided that she wanted our daughter to move back in with her. Ultimately it was my daughter's decision to make, and one I had hoped wouldn't be made in haste.

Believing that everything was all better, my daughter chose to go back and live with her mother. I was disappointed, not just that my daughter wouldn't be around as much, but because I knew all too well what would happen if her and her mother continued down the same path. Much like with my parents, without communication or some sort of reconciliation of the past, nothing would ever truly be resolved.

I often felt helpless in dealing with situations that would arise with my daughters when anything happened under their mother's roof. Without any communication or real co-parenting, there was never any way of knowing what was going on there. From what I could tell though, my ex always seemed to be angry with at least one of our daughters at any given time. Getting along as sisters had always been difficult for the two of them because they were constantly pitted against one another.

One of my biggest regrets was not paying closer attention to my oldest during that time. I was so fixated on making sure my youngest was getting what she needed that my oldest must have felt like an afterthought, something that couldn't have been further from the truth. She was always able to handle issues she had with her mother, and I guess I didn't worry about her as much because she always seemed to hold her own. It doesn't excuse not having the foresight to know that she'd need support too. I knew that the new situation was hurting her as well, and I'll always regret not knowing if she needed me. Despite everything, my oldest daughter and I were always close, and I was thrilled when she asked me to help her figure out her future after high school.

We had dinner out one night where we talked about her options. In front of me sat a beautiful, intelligent, and mature young woman asking me of all people for advice, which was crazy, because she was more mature than me in almost every way. I did my best to just listen and help her discover for herself what she'd like to pursue. She felt that her options were limited because of financing issues but I insisted that she find something that made her happy. An amazingly talented artist, my daughter had always really loved interior design, so when she decided on that as a career, I tried to find ways to support her when she went off to school.

Everything seemed to be going well for me. That summer I was busy at work and had a much better income, and best of all, I'd found a new apartment back in downtown Toronto. In fact, I had just finished moving myself in when my ex called to let me know that my youngest was coming to live with me once again. As I'd predicted, emotions had begun to run high in her household and as a result, my youngest was going to need some support.

Once again, I was more than happy to have my daughter come live with me although, my new living situation made it challenging. Being downtown Toronto meant that my daughter would have to be pulled out of her suburban high school in her senior year and made to attend a new inner-city school where she'd have no friends, and hardly any support. Not to mention, there'd be two of us living in a one-bedroom apartment, quite far from an ideal situation.

First and foremost, I needed to be sure that my daughter understood that no matter what, she was loved, and that we would figure out how to move forward. History often repeats itself, and there I was again holding my youngest child while she cried, asking me why her mother didn't love her.

Once again, my heart was broken, and what's more, at that point, I really had no answer for her. It was almost too much for me to bear, that all too familiar scene of rejection, and pain.

After careful consideration, I'd decided that my daughter deserved to spend her senior year of high school with her friends and in familiar surroundings, but because the waiting list for the building I was living in was over 3 years long, moving out just wasn't an option. In the end, I managed to find a temporary place for my youngest to stay during weekdays. A lovely older woman who was empty nesting was offering room and board in her home. It was a short walk to my daughter's school, and in close proximity to some of her friends. In order to pay for it, I went back to serving at the restaurant where I'd worked while I was in school. Any of the days where I wasn't working at the massage clinic, I would take a shift at the restaurant. Having two jobs again made me incredibly busy, but I really hoped my girls would understand that I was working hard to make sure that I could provide them with anything they needed.

At the end of the school year, when my youngest was graduating from high school, my oldest daughter and I went to the ceremony to cheer her on. I sat there in the school auditorium beaming with pride at how well she'd done despite the obstacles she'd been forced to overcome.

My ex attended the graduation as well, and though I felt no animosity towards her, we didn't really communicate. The last time we spoke, I'd been pretty vocal about what I thought of her as a parent, so it was no surprise that the reception she'd given me was a frosty one.

At the end of the ceremony, as we gathered outside to take pictures with the other parents and teachers, I noticed my ex off to one side on her phone. My heart sank as I realized that she didn't know any of the people around her. She hadn't really been involved in what was happening in her daughter's life and it made me sad to think how there'd be no way for her to get back the time that she'd lost.

With both my daughters now finished high school, and off to new adventures, I was able to reflect on what kind of relationship I had with them. Nothing I did was perfect, but I did the best I could with only their best interests at heart. There were reasons for every decision I'd made, and I acknowledge that they came with consequences.

For a lot of my childhood, I'd felt undeserving of love and affection, but I managed to foster the kind of relationship with my daughters that left them – and me – feeling loved unconditionally.

Being so open with my girls, I decided to get them together to discuss my less-than-stellar personal life, which had a history of being overly complicated. They'd always expressed their concern over my substandard screening process when it came to dating, and I wanted to let them know that it was something I'd been working on. By that time, I had been in a relationship with someone for several months, and things were going so well that I was finally ready to let them know.

I was very nervous, but it came as no surprise to me that after hearing that I'd been dating a man, they were overjoyed for me. They could see I was happy, and wanted nothing but the best for me. Of course, I could have done without hearing that my news had sanctioned the payout of a bet that had been made between the two of them.

Similar to the moment when I realized I belonged on the stage, I once again felt as though I was exactly who and where I needed to be. Living through the trauma of foster care, teen homelessness, and sexual abuse all had a lasting effect that could have forced me into a much darker existence. Instead, it fuelled my desire to forge my own path that led to numerous successes. There were bumps along the way to be sure, with a constant push by others, trying to force me to become something other than myself. Whether it was being told not to act too black, or that I wasn't acting black enough, or having to hide being queer, I refused to give up my identity to join the status quo.

I was able to overcome the pain of an ugly divorce, and my consequent battle with substance abuse, only to find myself a new career, and the opportunity to raise two amazingly well-adjusted daughters.

I was a survivor. And although I was never one to overstate my life and career, I'd learned that it's okay to admit that I'd accomplished amazing things despite the odds.

16

UNEXPECTED SONG

Getting up from the kitchen table, I reached to turn on the lights in the dining room. The sun was slowly fading behind our house, and if I was going to finish looking through old report cards from elementary school, I'd need to be able to see.

Grabbing at what I thought were the last of my old school reports, I came across something that had been wedged near the bottom of the box.

"What is that?" my mum asked as she struggled to see what I'd been trying to pry out from where it had been stuck. As it loosened, the newspaper wrapping tore off in my hand, exposing the wood of a picture frame. Pulling it from the other end, I managed to dislodge it, but the sound of breaking glass could be heard as it came free. I peeled back the rest of the paper, but could barely see the photo through the shards.

"Fuck," she said.

Hearing my mother utter such language made me instantly smile. It had always been her favourite word, but I hadn't heard it in quite some time. That was my mother, raw and unfiltered.

"Don't worry Mum, we can just replace the glass." I handed her the frame so she could get a better look. She stared at the photo with intense focus, and the longer she looked, the more I began to see the veil of her unbreakable fortitude begin to fall.

Pretending not to see that she was clearly upset, I gently took the picture from her and started to remove the broken pieces from the frame. The photo was one of me and my daughters that had been taken on a Disney Cruise several Christmases earlier. It was the first family photo we'd taken after I'd split up with my wife, and it was quite a difficult time for all three of us. I'd used the photo for Christmas cards that year, but had this one enlarged for my mum which she framed and placed on display in the living room.

"It's okay, Mum, the photo is fine." I shook the remaining smaller pieces of glass into the dust bin, and tried to distract her by changing the subject.

"You know, I understand now how difficult kids are, and I'm not exactly sure I gave you enough credit."

When I handed the frame back to her, she remained fixated on the image of my family. The expression on our faces in that picture showed us desperately trying to look unphased by the continuous emotional upset of the divorce.

"I know I didn't make things easy for you, in fact I was downright terrible. I'd been so overwhelmed by my emotions and unable to control them, that I fought you tooth and nail on almost everything, especially when it came to expressing myself. I need you to know that as angry and destructive as I was, it still hurt me when you dismissed my feelings as unimportant, simply because you couldn't relate."

I don't know what made me choose that exact moment to express those feelings, and I was worried how my mum was going to react. Her expression made it seem as though she had something she wanted to say but struggled to form the words. I could have simply left it there, but I felt compelled to continue on.

"As well intentioned as you were," I said, "when it came to my sense of identity, I felt as though you'd lost sight of what I needed from you most, which was your support. When I left home, I felt completely abandoned, and unloved, and it was one of the most difficult periods in my life."

I decided to spare her the details of the things I'd endured while homeless. Besides, I felt I'd done a pretty good job of making my point.

"We didn't know what to do, or how to handle you" my mum replied. "We just did what we thought was best for you." My mum was never one to admit that she didn't have all the answers. She would often try to explain away any of her decisions that didn't generate her desired result.

"I know you did," I told her, "and I understand."

I know that my parents really did try to help me, but I don't think that they were equipped to handle my emotional struggles that were the result of a traumatic past.

My mum was suddenly quiet, and seemed intent on listening to me without further interruption.

I had been ashamed of who I was for a multitude of reasons, not the least of which was my behaviour during my adolescence. I'd put my family through hell and yet, not to minimize what had happened, I was still just a kid. A kid who'd felt unwanted for so long that understandably, I never really got over it.

"We never really addressed any serious issues, so I was forced to bottle up all my pain and anger which I then took out on you simply because you were there. I know you, and I know that you've carried around a sense of having failed me, but you shouldn't. I'm happy with my life, and how I got here has a lot to do with you, and for that, I'll always be grateful."

These were feelings that I'd felt the need express for quite some time, and being able to share them with my mum was overwhelmingly liberating.

***

Finally, my dad gingerly made his way down the stairs, as he was prone to do since his legs had become weaker in his later years.

"Hey guy," he said, which was his usual way of greeting me. "Did you get a beer?"

"I'm okay," I answered. "I've got ginger ale."

He paused when he got to the landing at the bottom of the staircase at the front door. Then, straightening himself up, he made his way down the last two steps into the living room.

"You alright?" I asked.

"I'm fine, I'm fine," he murmured. "I'm not quite dead yet."

My dad made his way to the fridge to grab a beer, and passing the dining table he noticed what I'd been working at while he was upstairs.

"You got into it already, eh?"

The lump I felt in my throat prevented me from answering.

"What's wrong?" he asked.

"Nothing Dad, it's just a lot more than I'd anticipated."

I looked at the box and the two piles I'd created next to it. One contained the things I felt were important to me and sparked memories I wanted to hold onto. The other was full of duplicate photos and newspaper clippings as well as the things that triggered memories of things I'd chosen to forget.

"You should have waited for me to come down. I could have helped you with it."

Sitting down across the table from me, my dad took a sip of his beer, and let out a huge sigh, like a lazy dog sitting in the hot summer sun.

"Are you okay?" I asked him.

"Yeah, I'm fine. I just miss her, ya know."

"I know you do Dad."

I looked over at my mum's favourite chair and half expected to see her sitting there, but the chair remained as empty as it had been these past two years. So a wave of sadness and regret washed over me as I tried to hold onto the image of her face in my mind.

As strange as it seemed, I still felt her presence whenever I thought of her, which was often. It was comforting to think of her as being near, especially when family was together.

Pushing the box aside, I wondered how my dad had really been doing. He had been my mum's primary caregiver, and the stress had definitely taken its toll on him.

"Can you believe the snow we had that year?" I asked, trying to steer the conversation to something slightly less solemn. "I always blamed Mum for that."

I had driven through a full-on blizzard up to the cottage when she passed, and I was convinced she had been responsible for it. I laughed out loud as I suggested that the storm was my mum's final "fuck you" to us all. My dad laughed too.

"You know, I didn't expect you to be overly sentimental about any of this stuff," I told him.

"What do you mean?" he asked.

I held up a playbill from a recent Toronto production of *Cats*, for which I'd come out of retirement to play Old Deuteronomy. Watching that show was the first time my dad had ever seen me in something without my mum, and I think that out of habit, he saved the playbill which is what my mum would have done.

"Oh yeah," he said. "It was weird watching you perform without her."

"In what way?" I asked.

"Well, Mum always used to squeeze my hand really tight as soon as she'd see you onstage."

I laughed at the idea of it.

"She would always get so nervous for you. She was afraid you'd forget your words or something."

I couldn't believe that after all that time, she still felt that way. It wasn't like I was in a high school production, I had been a professional for years. Even so, I suppose none of that matters when it's your kid up there.

When my mum was diagnosed with ALS, she had some time to prepare for the end. My box was one of three that she'd put together, one for each of her kids. Each one filled with random items that she'd considered important to keep. I figured I'd find mine filled with some old Christmas cards, or macaroni art I'd made in first grade. What I hadn't expected was a carefully detailed documentary of my life.

The relationship I'd had with my mother had been complicated, and based on arguments fuelled by our differing opinions, but we did love each other. We were both very strong-willed, and we both had staunch beliefs that didn't necessarily complement one another.

All those photos and letters that I hadn't seen in years had made me realize what I'd lost after she'd gone. My mum never talked about things that were overly emotional, and even though she'd never actually said the words to me, the stockpile of evidence stored in this one little box was indisputable proof that my mum had been proud of me.

I'm not sure if I'd have said all the things I imagined saying to her had she still been alive, but I'd like to think I would have, if only to have the two of us share some truly honest sentiments. Revisiting emotions of the past was therapeutic, and because it was her idea to create that box of memories, I figured it was for her as well.

My mum was a woman with a huge heart, and although for years I had resented her, thinking she hadn't provided me what I needed to succeed in life, I was still able to let go of any pain or anger, and simply love her for trying.

I contemplated sharing my feelings about the past with my dad, but it most certainly wouldn't have ended very well. Anytime I'd even hinted at the possibility that some of his past behaviours had been even a little problematic, he would instantly get defensive.

My father really struggled with admitting to himself any role he may have played in things that happened to me when I was younger. I was the source of so much of his stress and I'm not even sure that I'd know how to deal with a child that was like me; so completely wrought with sadness, pain, and anger. Regardless, when confronted about his temper or how he chose to handle certain situations with me, his pre-emptive assertion of, "I didn't do anything," made for a fairly unconvincing defence. That was classic of my dad though.

In his heart of hearts, he knew what he'd done. He knew that he was responsible for saying and doing things that left me feeling rejected, and so I decided to let him continue that little bit of denial, which seemed to be what made him feel most comfortable.

My dad got up from his chair, and as I watched him struggle to put out food for the cat, I noticed that he'd accidently dropped some onto the floor. I was shocked that he didn't try to clean it up, but as I looked around the kitchen, I noticed that it hadn't been the first time either. In fact, as I'd scanned the room again, I began to realize that the house was nowhere as clean as I'd originally thought. I went to grab a rag from the kitchen sink to wipe up the spill when my dad, casually sitting back down in his chair, told me not to bother.

"Don't worry," he said to me. "Your sister will get it."

"What are you talking about?" I asked.

Because my sister lived closest to him, she would stop by to check in on him two or three times a week, always ready to help him with whatever he needed.

"You know, you're perfectly capable of doing things for yourself," I challenged, with the understanding that he knew what he was doing. When I spoke to him, I made sure to look directly into his eyes, making sure not to shift my gaze under any circumstance.

Usually, anytime I was around my dad, I would revert right back to an eight-year-old boy; the same one who was terrified of handing him the wrong wrench while helping him work on his car. For some reason though, in this moment, I didn't feel the same way.

Because I'd always assumed that he'd seen me as a lost cause when I was a teen, I spent my life chasing success as a way to prove my father wrong. I thought that if I could just show him that I was special, he'd regret having given up on me. My intense focus on delivering some sort of divine retribution prevented me from seeing that my father hadn't actually abandoned me at all. He did what he felt he had to do, and sending me away wasn't easy for him. I wasn't there to see the man who was pacing back and forth around the house at night, crying because he didn't know where I was or what was happening to me. At the time, all I could think about were the nights I spent on the streets, and the predator in the shelter with his hands down my pants. I'd wasted so much time feeling angry and betrayed, that I never saw how much he suffered too.

"Look Dad, I understand that it's difficult for you with Mum gone, but there's nothing wrong with you. You need to start taking care of yourself, and waiting for people to do everything for you isn't helping."

I didn't actually change the subject, I just gently doubled down on how I felt about his antics.

"Okay," he said, and that was the end of it.

I placed the lid back on the bankers' box which now contained only things I'd decided to keep, and placed it on the stairs near the front door with some other items that I was taking home.

Sitting back down at the dining table, I continued to finish my soda as my father drank his beer. He continued to talk about random things. How the doctor had put him on a new medication that was helping his legs, and how he'd started exercising at the

Jewish Community Centre twice a week. Nothing of great urgency, mostly just small talk.

"Hey guy, you want something to eat before you go?" he asked.

"No, I'm okay. Thanks, though."

I knew that my husband would be cooking dinner, and I was hoping to make it home at a reasonable hour.

Then, there was an odd moment of silence between us, which was broken by something I didn't expect.

"I love this you know," he blurted out. "I love when the two of us just sit and talk."

I had no idea how to respond. This was something very different from him, and I think that my lack of preparedness left me a little confused about my feelings.

"Ya know, I've always admired how you could always be yourself, no matter what life would throw at you."

What he said caused me to feel that all-too-familiar lump in my throat. It was difficult to hold back my urge to cry, as I struggled to seem unaffected.

I was an emotional wreck. Anger, sadness, happiness…all the feelings, all at once. Why was he saying this to me now? After years of being so demonstratively resentful of the man, here he was, being uncharacteristically reflective and sentimental. Maybe he'd always felt this way, but I couldn't possibly know because he'd never actually said the words. And although I couldn't help but wish that he'd revealed this sentiment to me years earlier, there it was.

"Thanks, I enjoy talking to you too," I said.

I got up from the table and slowly gathered things to load into my car, making sure to take my time while I thought about this surprisingly sudden and strange interaction.

On the surface, it appeared as though things remained status quo and although we'd never really talked about the past, the fact that he was suddenly speaking so unreservedly, indicated at the very least that there had been some sort of introspection. Still, I couldn't seem to figure out my dad's sudden sensibility, so I decided to just accept it for what it was.

I walked back to where my father was standing by the front door. "Same time next week?"

My father nodded and gave me a thumbs-up.

"Just let me know if you need anything else in the meantime."

I turned to walk back to the car, but was halted by the sudden urge to add another sentiment. "Oh, and Dad, thanks for hanging onto all this stuff. It really means a lot to me."

"Love you guy," he said, and gave me a strong hug.

There was something in the way he held onto me. My whole life, I'd wanted to feel like this. Of course he'd hugged me many times in the past, but now that I'd finally let go of a lifetime of anger and shame, I could finally accept it wholeheartedly. Now, in this one embrace, we shared a mutual sense of vulnerability.

"Love you too, Dad."

Walking back to the car, I opened the driver's side door, and got in. I was overcome by a sense of being shut off from the rest of the world in the eerie silence that happens just before starting your car's engine. I took that moment to revel in a slight sense of pride. It was a promising start to what would become weekly visits with my dad, where the hard lines between us would soften, and our relationship would become stronger.

Forgiveness is choosing freedom, but its institution isn't one-size-fits-all. It's possible to be angry, and at the same time, choose to forgive. And although I'd felt differently for years, it wasn't just my father I needed to forgive, it was myself. I'd spent so much time being angry at my parents for everything they *hadn't* given me, that I lost sight of everything they *had*.

With my father, because saying as much would imply he'd done something wrong, and it would therefore be met with emphatic refutation, I decided I would keep the words "I forgive you" to myself. After all, I was never going to get an apology, and to be honest, I didn't need one. Hearing the words at this stage of our relationship wouldn't necessarily make me like him more, and not hearing them wouldn't make me love him any less.

As I headed home to Toronto listening to my usual music playlist, I turned up the volume when I heard the song *Landslide* by Fleetwood Mac. It was one of my favourite songs by one of my favourite bands, and it was the song that my daughters and I had sung for my mother just weeks before she died. That was the first time I'd ever seen my father cry, and listening to it now, I too was brought to tears. Songs like this not only reminded me of my mum, they reminded me of some of the most difficult times in my life. They were the pain I endured, and the sorrow I felt. They were every moment of my life when it was suggested that it would be better to be someone else, rather than myself.

They were also a reminder of the happier moments. Beams of light peeking through the dark cloud that seemed to follow me around. Those little breaks in the storm that gave me the strength to maintain my authenticity while following my dreams. This, rather than becoming what I felt I'd been set up to become: Uninspiring, Uninteresting, and Uncoloured.